Do They Exist?

Do Ghosts Exist?

Hal Marcovitz

ReferencePoint Press®

San Diego, CA

About the Author
Hal Marcovitz is a former newspaper reporter and columnist who makes his home in Chalfont, Pennsylvania. He is the author of more than 170 books for young readers.

© 2016 ReferencePoint Press, Inc.
Printed in the United States

For more information, contact:
ReferencePoint Press, Inc.
PO Box 27779
San Diego, CA 92198
www.ReferencePointPress.com

Picture Credits:
Cover: Fer Gregory/Shutterstock.com; © Corbis: 6; Depositphotos: 25; © Everett Historical/Shutterstock.com: 16, 56; MGM/Dimension/Photofest: 61; © Reno Martin/Shutterstock.com: 10; Paramount Pictures/Photofest: 34; Public Health England/Science Photo Library: 44; George Skene/MCT/Newscom: 41; Thinkstock Images: 21, 50, 66; The Ghost of Banquo (oil on canvas), Chasseriau, Theodore (1819–56)/Musee des Beaux-Arts, Reims, France/Bridgeman Images: 31

LIBRARY OF CONGRESS CATALOGING-IN-PUBLICATION DATA

Marcovitz, Hal.
  Do ghosts exist? / by Hal Marcovitz.
    pages cm. -- (Do they exist?)
  Includes bibliographical references and index.
  Audience: Grade 9 to 12.
  ISBN-13: 978-1-60152-856-8 (hardback)
  ISBN-10: 1-60152-856-6 (hardback) 1. Ghosts--Juvenile literature. I. Title.
  BF1461.M357 2016
  133.1--dc23
                                                                    2015013412

Contents

Ghost Hunting: Science or Pseudoscience?

Magician and escape artist Harry Houdini was an enormously popular entertainer during the early years of the twentieth century. His daring escapes—freeing himself from handcuffs while dangling from bridges, escaping from padlocked jail cells or trunks submerged in rivers—all made headlines and earned him legions of fans. But Houdini never claimed to have accomplished these amazing feats through supernatural abilities. Houdini readily admitted that his techniques were drawn from sleight-of-hand skills.

At one point in his career Houdini grew interested in ghosts and wondered whether it is possible to communicate with the spirits of the dead. He attended several séances—ceremonies in which mediums attempt to communicate with ghosts. A medium is a person who claims to have the power to make contact with spirits. During the typical séance the spirit of a dead person supposedly speaks through the voice of the medium.

After attending several séances Houdini became convinced that mediums were frauds, charging clients high fees for the promise of communicating with deceased loved ones. In his book *A Magician Among the Spirits* he writes,

> I have gone to investigate . . . but as a result of my efforts I must confess that I am farther than ever from

belief in the genuineness of the Spirit manifestations and after twenty-five years of ardent research and endeavor I declare that nothing has been revealed to convince me that intercommunication has been established between the Spirits of the departed and those still in the flesh.[1]

Believing in Ghosts

Houdini dedicated himself to exposing fraudulent mediums. He joined a committee established by *Scientific American* magazine and wrote extensively about phony mediums whom he accused of cheating grieving relatives out of their money. One case he described involved a colleague, William Crookes, who exposed medium Florence Cook as a fake. Crookes attended a séance in which the medium claimed to have summoned the ghost of a woman named Katie King. During the séance, which was held in a darkened room, Crookes felt a woman take his arm. He described what happened next:

> "Nothing has been revealed to convince me that intercommunication has been established between the Spirits of the departed and those still in the flesh."[1]
>
> —*Magician and escape artist Harry Houdini.*

Several times she took my arm and the impression I received that it was a living woman at my side and not a visitor from the other world was so strong . . . I asked permission to take her in my arms. . . . This permission was graciously given, and I took advantage of it respectfully, as any gentleman would have done in the same circumstances. The "ghost," which made no resistance, was a being as material as Miss Cook herself.[2]

The campaign by Houdini, Crookes, and others dedicated to exposing fraudulent mediums made many headlines, but despite their efforts people have continued to harbor belief in ghosts and the ability to communicate with the dead. Indeed, a 2013 poll

Well-known magician and escape artist Harry Houdini poses for a photo before a performance. After he became interested in the subject of ghosts, Houdini investigated mediums—individuals who claim to be able to communicate with the dead—and concluded that they were frauds.

commissioned by the *Huffington Post* online newspaper found an astounding number of Americans—45 percent—believe in ghosts. That statistic reflects the belief of nearly 150 million people. Moreover, 28 percent of the people interviewed for the poll said they had *actually seen* a ghost. Another 13 percent said they may have seen a ghost—but were not sure.

The Science of Ghost Hunting

Mediums can still be found at work in the twenty-first century. But others who seek contact with spirits have emerged as well. Experts who probe the paranormal, using scientific instruments, crisscross the country delving into reports of hauntings. One tool used by the paranormal investigator is the night-vision scope, which enables the wearer to see light emitted in the infrared spectrum. Human eyes see only a fraction of the light that is emitted by the sun; light emitted in the infrared spectrum is invisible to the naked eye but can be detected with specially equipped cameras and other instruments. Says paranormal investigator Jason Hawes, cofounder of The Atlantic Paranormal Society (TAPS),

> In every investigation, we collect a wealth of data through different types of cameras, meters, and voice recorders, and from observations and reports of strange experiences. We sift through all of this as objectively as possible before we begin to draw conclusions. We understand that ghost hunting isn't an exact science. We have to accept the fact that we are working in a real-world setting. However, we are determined to come as close to scientific accuracy as we possibly can. That's the only way we are going to produce reliable evidence and advance the study of the paranormal.[3]

There are, however, many scientists and others whose notions regarding the validity of paranormal investigation can be summed up with a single word: nonsense. They insist that ghosts are figments of people's imaginations, and whatever scientific evidence paranormal investigators think they are accumulating can be easily debunked. Says clinical psychologist Jonathan C. Smith, "Every careful scientific examination of dark moving shapes in abandoned houses has found an alternative to the ghost explanation. Dark moving shapes are routinely found to be shadows of objects like drapes, reflections of moving lights, or rodents."[4]

"We are determined to come as close to scientific accuracy as we possibly can. That's the only way we are going to produce reliable evidence and advance the study of the paranormal."[3]

—Paranormal investigator Jason Hawes.

Smith and others label the work of ghost hunters like Hawes *pseudoscience*—essentially, the misinterpretation of scientific data to explain a theory or assumption. The earliest form of pseudoscience was probably alchemy—the ancient belief that the chemical makeup of metals such as lead could be altered into gold. Still, skeptics such as Smith have not stopped believers like Hawes from continuing their work investigating the paranormal. As the *Huffington Post* poll suggests, in modern times many people are as willing to believe in the existence of ghosts as they were a century ago when Houdini campaigned to prove the impossibility of communicating with the dead.

Chapter 1

What Are Ghosts?

"Poltergeists have disturbed humans throughout history. An Ancient Egyptian scribe recorded a violent attack in which the beds of the household shook and stones showered out of the air."

—Alasdair Wickham, British writer and paranormal expert.

Alasdair Wickham, *The Dead Roam the Earth: True Stories of the Paranormal from Around the World*. New York: Penguin, 2012, p. 93.

"Poltergeist reports are based entirely on eyewitness testimony. The case for their reality as anything other than teenage pranks is exceeding poor."

—Terence Hines, professor of neurology at Pace University, New York City.

Terence Hines, *Pseudoscience and the Paranormal*. Amherst, NY: Prometheus, 2003, p. 98.

For there to be a belief in ghosts, there must first be a belief that in every person a spirit exists in which all the non-physical characteristics of the person reside: the demeanor, sense of humor, intelligence, emotions of love and hate, and so on. When death arrives, and the physical body ceases to function, the spirit of the person—the ghost—leaves the body and continues to exist. "The solid, dense energy of our physical body begins to deteriorate," says paranormal expert James Van Praagh. "The light, transparent energy body that is an exact replica of the physical body emerges and moves into the spirit worlds."[5]

Popular culture has often portrayed ghosts as appearing as though they are draped in white bedsheets. Such notions are

Although ghosts are often depicted as white forms like the one shown here, paranormal researchers say that spirits come in all shapes and sizes—even in the form of ghost pets.

usually confined to Halloween fun houses and images of Casper, the friendly ghost—a familiar character found in comic books, cartoons, and animated films for decades.

But paranormal investigators, as well as people who have claimed to have seen ghosts, are convinced they appear in many forms. Says Leo Ruickbie, a British historian who specializes in the study of the paranormal, "White ladies, green ladies, blue ladies, headless horsemen, as well as coachmen, drummer-boys, underground pipers, marching soldiers, fighting armies, phantom coaches, ghost trains, spectral pets—all these and more are the sorts of spirits that people believe have come back from the dead or the past to haunt us."[6]

Apparitions

Regardless of whether the ghost appears as a green lady or headless horseman, all the images described by Ruickbie are known as apparitions. An apparition is an appearance of the actual embodiment of the deceased person—although, as Ruickbie suggests, the apparition may or may not be accompanied by a head. A typical apparition was discovered by a young woman named Donna as she walked along the beach in the New Jersey resort community of Cape May. The apparition seen by Donna was not green, and it did have its head, but she discovered other quirky behaviors as she observed the ghost:

> All I remember is that there was this old-looking man up ahead, maybe twenty feet, standing at the crest of a little rise, looking right toward me, but somehow right past me.
>
> It was as if he didn't know I was there. I stared right at the figure and could make out certain details. The sun was just coming up, and you could start to see the colors of the day and whatnot, but this man, this figure, was a little unusual. It didn't seem to have any color. It was a pale gray, and almost glowing. It seemed to have the light that you get when you put one of those phosphorescent keychains or whatever under a bright light and then watch it glow-in-the-dark. It wasn't bright but it was very noticeable.[7]

Donna says she took a few steps closer to the apparition and noticed his unusual clothes: His pants were tattered, and instead of a belt he wore a sash. He also wore a T-shirt that Donna observed was dirty and tattered. The man turned to her and chuckled. And then, she says,

> He slowly turned around, and started to walk. Well, as I re-member, it was not so much a walk, but more like a coast. It was just like, and I hate to say this because it sounds so silly, but it was just like you'd imagine some ghost movie. He moved without moving his legs, if you can picture that. The figure just glided, up and over the hill, and disappeared. It was really strange.[8]

Donna approached the crest where the apparition had been standing. She describes what happened next:

> There, halfway between me and the water, was the man, well, the ghost. It was coasting or gliding smoothly over the sand toward the water. And, in the distance, I could hear that whispering or giggling sound. . . . I followed that figure as it slowly went toward the water, and I wondered what would happen next. Well, it didn't take long. The fig-ure went up, closer and closer to the water, and eventually just went right in the water. It just kept on gliding until it was knee-deep, then shoulder-deep, and then all the way in the water. That was the last I saw of it.[9]

Ghostly Images

Apparitions can be found in a number of varieties. The atmo-spheric apparition is typically seen in one place only, repeating the same task over and over again—usually an act connected to a traumatic event. The ghost of someone who died in an airplane crash, for instance, may be seen repeatedly sitting in an airport lounge, waiting for the doomed flight to be called. Another version of the apparition is the deathbed ghost. As the name suggests, a deathbed ghost appears at the moment of death, rising from the physical body of the deceased person.

Ghosts of Animals

Believers in the paranormal suggest that an apparition does not have to appear to be human—people have reported seeing apparitions of deceased pets. The existence of the spirits of animals was suggested as early as 1913 by Elliott O'Donnell, an author and paranormal expert. "The mere fact that there are manifestations of dead people proves some kind of life after death for human beings; and happily the same proof is available with regard for a future life for animals; indeed, there are as many animal phantoms as human—perhaps more," said O'Donnell.

In 2004 Mike and Renee Leppard found a stray kitten near their Texas home. Although the Leppards already provided a home for five cats, they adopted the kitten, naming him Scampers. One night Renee was awakened by Scampers, who seemed to be playing with another, though unseen, cat. Scampers swatted at the air with his paw and tumbled around. Then he chased the unseen cat.

Soon the other cats in the house joined in the play. In each case the cats seemed to engage in typical play common among cats—except there did not seem to be another cat involved. Says paranormal investigator Dusty Rainbolt, "It's something to behold when the cats begin to chase the invisible cat in different directions, leaping, stretching and vocalizing. . . . Renee used to think the melee was the cats' morning wake-up call for their breakfast, but rarely are the food dishes empty when this occurs. Now, she believes the ghost cat gets them stirred up."

Quoted in Dusty Rainbolt, *Ghost Cats: Human Encounters with Feline Spirits.* Guilford, CT: Lyons, 2007, p. 2.

Rainbolt, *Ghost Cats: Human Encounters with Feline Spirits,* p. 37.

A most common form of apparition is the ghost that appears in a photograph. The apparition was not evident when the photographer peered into the viewfinder, but when the photo was printed or viewed on a screen, the apparition's image had been captured. Scottish paranormal investigator Gordon Rutter describes a case of an apparition caught on film by a woman who photographed the ghost in an Edinburgh hotel room. He recalls that the woman was getting ready for an evening with her friends when she decided to take a few photographs of her hotel room as a memento. When she later looked at the processed photos, she noticed what appeared be an image of a woman in the window. Because the room was on the second floor, however, it would have been impossible for someone to be standing outside the window. Rutter adds,

> The photographer was alone in the room and it's not her reflection as she is blonde and the figure is dark haired, these are not the clothes she was wearing and her camera cannot be seen. The figure is wearing a white maid's cap, but [the] photograph was taken just before the group went out for the evening, so there shouldn't have been any maids around—particularly not outside the window of [the] room.

> The figure appears to be either reflected in the window or on the other side of the window rather than superimposed over it or between the photographer and the window. If it's a reflected person, painting or television, then these objects would have to be very large indeed. An impressive and intriguing picture.[10]

Grey Ladies

Another form of apparition is the grey lady (usually spelled *grey* rather than *gray*), the ghost of a woman who died of a broken heart. A grey lady is said to haunt Gainsborough Old Hall, a five-hundred-year-old manor house in Lincolnshire, a rural district of England along the North Sea coast. Local legend suggests the grey lady is the ghost of a young woman whose family lived in the manor house during the Tudor era, a reign of British monarchs that spanned from the late 1400s to early 1600s. Historians have never been able to identify the grey lady, but it is believed she fell in love with a soldier and that the couple planned to elope. Her father, the lord of the manor, opposed the union, and when he discovered the couple's plans he imprisoned his daughter in one of the manor's towers. She pined away in the tower, finally dying of a broken heart.

Visitors to the manor have reported seeing the apparition of a young woman gliding down a corridor, her long dress trailing behind her. Always, at the end of the corridor the ghost makes a right turn and then disappears through a wall. During a renovation of the manor house in the 1960s, workers broke through the wall and discovered it had been erected to hide a doorway. "Legend states it is the doorway the Grey Lady comes through, looking for her forbidden lover,"[11] says British historian Susanna O'Neill.

In America, another grey lady is said to haunt Riverwood, a mansion in Nashville, Tennessee, erected in 1795. This grey lady has been identified as Martha Wilson Porter, who died in 1860 shortly after learning that her husband-to-be had died in a logging accident. In 1984 historian Grace Benedict Paine wrote of this incident at Riverwood:

> Suddenly, without warning, the bridge cards flew into the air from Miss Sadie's hands. "Pshaw, it's just the 'gray lady,'" she reassured her startled guests in the grand antebellum mansion, Riverwood. "She has been our family ghost since my relative, Judge Cooper, bought the house over a hundred years ago." Miss Sadie and her husband, Dr. Lucius E. Burch, had grown quite used to the sudden appearances and activities of the apparition during the years they had lived in Riverwood.[12]

Lincoln's Ghost

The apparitions that haunt Gainsborough Old Hall and Riverwood seem to have stepped out of the pages of history, although their stories are not widely known or studied. One very famous historical figure whose ghost has been reported many times is Abraham

President Abraham Lincoln (pictured) was assassinated shortly after the end of the Civil War. Since then many people, including the daughter and son-in-law of President Ronald Reagan, have reported encountering Lincoln's ghost in the White House.

Lincoln. The ghost of the president, assassinated in 1865, is believed by some to roam the halls of the White House in Washington, DC.

In the 1920s Grace Coolidge, the wife of then US president Calvin Coolidge, claimed to have seen Lincoln's apparition staring out a White House window. Other notables of the time who said they had witnessed Lincoln's ghost in the White House were Queen Wilhelmina of the Netherlands; First Lady Eleanor Roosevelt's maid Mary Eban; and Winston Churchill, the prime minister of Great Britain.

In more recent times Maureen Reagan, the daughter of former US president Ronald Reagan, and her husband, Dennis Revell, believed they saw Lincoln's ghost while staying in the White House during the Reagan administration in the 1980s. First Lady Nancy Reagan relates in her memoirs what Maureen and Dennis told her:

> One night Dennis woke up and saw a shadowy figure by the fireplace. Maureen just laughed at him when he told her about it—until *she* woke up one night and saw a man who seemed to be wearing a red coat. At first she thought it was [President Reagan] in his bathrobe, but when she looked again she noticed that the figure was transparent! Maureen says he was staring out the window and then turned around to look at her before he vanished.[13]

Nancy Reagan says she never saw Lincoln's ghost, but on one occasion while inspecting the Lincoln Bedroom she noticed the portrait of Lincoln was crooked. When the First Lady told a maid that the portrait needed straightening, the maid responded, "Oh, he's been here again"[14]—meaning that Lincoln's ghost was apt to play tricks on the White House staff and had purposely tilted the portrait.

Cold Spots, Spirals, and Orbs

According to Maureen Reagan, Lincoln's apparition was transparent, and therefore she could easily tell she had seen a ghost. Sometimes, though, apparitions are said to look and act like a living person and are therefore not easily identifiable as ghosts. In fact, sometimes the ghosts themselves do not even know they are ghosts. They interact with the living and go about their business oblivious to the fact that they are dead. Says paranormal investigator Dave Juliano, "Some spirits remain at or near the site of their death, especially if it was sudden and unexpected. They remain confused and don't know or accept that they have died. These spirits remain in the area and try

> "Maureen says he was staring out the window and then turned around to look at her before he vanished."[13]
>
> —Nancy Reagan, former First Lady.

The Ghost of Willie Lincoln

Mary Todd Lincoln, the widow of President Abraham Lincoln, believed in ghosts and even held séances in the White House. Mrs. Lincoln's interest in the spirit world was prompted by the death of her son, Willie, in 1862. The boy was a victim of typhoid fever.

Lizzie Keckley, a friend of the First Lady, had also lost a son and found comfort in visiting Belle Miller, a Washington, DC, medium. Keckley encouraged Mary Lincoln to visit Miller. The First Lady eventually made many trips to Miller's home in Washington's Georgetown neighborhood, where she attempted to communicate with Willie. Historians believe President Lincoln accompanied the First Lady to the Miller home on several occasions.

Eventually, Mary Lincoln moved the séances into the White House, inviting friends as well as advisers to her husband to attend the sessions. She once told Charles Sumner, a senator from Massachusetts, "A very slight veil separates us from the loved and lost and to me there is comfort in the thought that though unseen by us they are very near."

Mary Lincoln believed she saw Willie's ghost in the White House. She also believed she saw the ghosts of former presidents Thomas Jefferson and John Tyler.

Quoted in Jean H. Baker, *Mary Lincoln: A Biography*. New York: Norton, 1989, p. 220.

to make contact with anyone that passes by that is sensitive to spirits. This type of spirit can be found almost anywhere a death has occurred."[15]

One sure way by which paranormal investigators can tell that a ghost is really a ghost is that the house haunted by the spirit often has what is known as a cold spot—a place within the home where the temperature is many degrees cooler than the rest of the house. Paranormal experts suggest the cold spot is an indication that a supernatural presence is drawing energy from within the home. Houses with cold spots often have funnel ghosts—

wisps or spirals of light in the shape of a swirl that can be found near the cold spot.

Similar to funnel ghosts are orbs: transparent or translucent balls of light that hover in the air. Orbs mostly show up in photographs—they cannot be seen by the naked eye, but their presence emerges on film or on digital images. An orb is believed to be the soul of a human that has left the body of the deceased and frequently remains in the room or home where the person died. But orbs have also been known to float from place to place. Some paranormal experts believe orbs eventually develop into full apparitions.

Vengeful Ghosts

In most cases apparitions do not intend to frighten people. They just look and act as they did in life. Certainly, though, the expression of fright is a common and understandable reaction of a person who believes he or she has seen a ghost—even one that means the person no harm. But many ghosts are believed to harbor evil intentions and to show up with the express purpose of frightening the living.

One type of ghost that harbors evil intentions is the vengeful ghost, a spirit that believes it has been wronged by a living person. Perhaps the victim of the vengeful ghost caused the death of the person whose spirit is now seeking vengeance. The vengeful ghost will return to haunt and torment the victim.

Sometimes the vengeful ghost has far more obscure reasons for tormenting its victim—and these reasons are known only to the ghost. In 1978 Jane Hartlein moved into a 261-year-old house in Liberty Corners, New Jersey. Hartlein is an antiques dealer and sells many antique dolls. Soon after moving into the home, Hartlein and her sister opened a box containing several dolls and noticed the eyes of all the dolls were missing. She says, "We pulled the dolls out and every doll that had once had glass eyes . . . the eyes had been plucked out. And there were no eyes on the bottom of the

"We pulled the dolls out and every doll that had once had glass eyes . . . the eyes had been plucked out. And there were no eyes on the bottom of the box."[16]

— Antiques dealer Jane Hartlein.

box."[16] Hartlein looked over the other dolls in her collection and found they were all missing their eyes.

Hartlein's sister did some investigating and learned from local residents that about two hundred years earlier a three-year-old girl had died in the home and was buried in a family cemetery on the grounds. The girl's ghost had remained in the home, Hartlein's sister was told. And according to what Hartlein's sister learned, the ghost harbored ill will toward toys because the girl had been denied the opportunity to play with her own dolls. That ill will may have led the ghost to remove the eyes of the dolls. "She might resent that I've got these antique toys," says Hartlein. "Maybe she feels they're her toys. Maybe she wants to destroy the toys, I don't know."[17]

Poltergeists

Of the ghosts that attempt to frighten the living, no ghost is said to have more malevolent intentions than the poltergeist. The term *poltergeist* has its roots in the combination of two German words: *polter*, which means to knock or make loud noises, and *geist*, which means ghost. Therefore, a poltergeist is a noisy ghost. But a poltergeist is much more than a noisy nuisance: A poltergeist is a ghost whose mischief is intended to frighten, cause harm, and even cause the death of its victim. "The poltergeist is a noisy, mischievous, destructive entity prone to acts of mindless violence,"[18] says paranormal investigator Brian Righi. The poltergeist's pranks may surface as unexplainable noises or objects that fly through the air, seemingly under their own power. Or the poltergeist may be responsible for other weird happenings—such as doors slamming or windows flying open without cause.

> "The poltergeist is a noisy, mischievous, destructive entity prone to acts of mindless violence."[18]
>
> —Paranormal investigator Brian Righi.

In 2006 a young married couple, Marc and Marianne, moved into a home in the town of South Shields in northeastern England. Soon after moving in, the couple says, the poltergeist made its presence known: The initials "RIP" appeared on a kitchen wall. (RIP are the initials for Rest In Peace, an inscription found on old tombstones.) Next, Marianne received texts on her phone stating

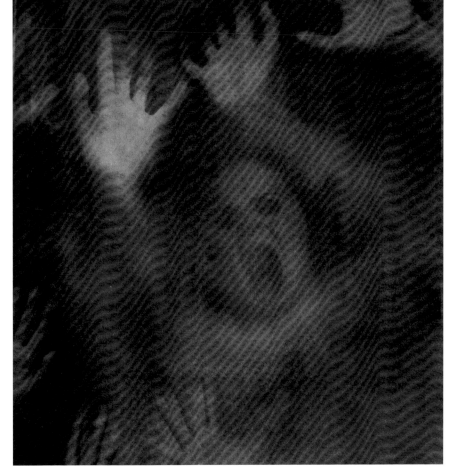

It is believed that most types of ghosts do not intend to frighten the living, but some do. Of these, poltergeists, whose name derives from German words meaning "noisy ghost," are the most malevolent. Poltergeists have been blamed for weird happenings capable of terrifying their living victims.

"Going to die today" and "I'll come for you when you are asleep."[19] Marianne tried to trace the texts, but there were no phone numbers of origination. Next, household objects started flying around the home. Strange sounds—bangs and cracks—could be heard. Marc caught sight of the poltergeist when he saw a dark shape in the form of a man, moving about the house. Marc says he felt a chill in the air as the poltergeist roamed from room to room. Occasionally, Marc felt a poking sensation in his back followed by a burning pain. Sometimes, for reasons he could not explain, scratches broke out on his skin, some of them so deep they bled.

It seemed to Marc and Marianne that as their reactions to the poltergeist's actions grew more fearful, the harder the poltergeist tried to frighten them. Says British writer and paranormal expert

Alasdair Wickham, "Poltergeists are drawn to people in emotional . . . flux. They feed off their energy, are partially shaped by their personality and grow into uncontrollable forces that create bizarre, frightening disturbances."[20] Perhaps the scariest incident occurred when the couple discovered their young son was not in his bed. After frantically searching the house, they found him asleep in a kitchen cupboard. The cupboard, fastened to a wall, was too high for the child to climb into himself.

After about a year, the paranormal activity ceased—evidently, the poltergeist moved on to find a new family to frighten. "The activity eventually petered out, but not before the couple's nerves had been shredded,"[21] says Wickham.

Skeptics Remain

Grey ladies, swirls, orbs, poltergeists, and other manifestations of ghosts are all members of a spirit world that many people insist exists. Over the years many people have given eyewitness accounts of ghosts such as those provided by Maureen Reagan or by Donna, the young woman from Cape May. Photographic evidence is surfacing in places such as the hotel in Edinburgh. And workers at Gainsborough Old Hall have uncovered a hidden door that could explain why the Lincolnshire grey lady always chooses a particular corridor for her frequent visits.

> "It is certainly a giant leap from a series of odd noises or a door swinging to a haunted house."[22]
>
> —Pace University professor Terence Hines.

And yet, skeptics remain unconvinced. "Most reports of hauntings . . . derive from far more mundane phenomena," insists Terence Hines, a professor of neurology at Pace University in New York City. "Strange moans, groans, knockings, and the like are heard. Or doors swing shut when no breeze was about. These are sometimes interpreted as being the work of a ghostly presence, even if an apparition is never seen. It is certainly a giant leap from a series of odd noises or a door swinging to a haunted house."[22]

As Hines suggests, there are many explanations for what would otherwise be regarded as ghostly phenomena. But those who believe they have seen ghosts or have been terrified by them may be unwilling to accept those explanations.

Chapter 2

Why Do People Believe in Ghosts?

"Suppose that death is, indeed, a journey to another place. Suppose the destination is as commonly imagined, and contains the spirits of all who have died. I ask you—what prospect matches that?"

—Socrates, fifth-century-BCE Greek philosopher.

Quoted in Nigel Spivey and Michael Squire, *Panorama of the Classical World*. London: Thames & Hudson, 2004, p. 16.

"Perhaps . . . we want to believe that our loved ones are not gone, or maybe we want to believe that we, too, won't just cease to exist one day. Whatever the reason, Satan is busy perpetrating the very first lie he ever told humankind: 'You will not certainly die.'"

—Heather Thompson Day, professor of communications at Southwestern Michigan College.

Heather Thompson Day, *The God Myth and Other Lies*. Hagerstown, MD: Review and Herald, 2014, p. 81.

The belief in ghosts has been a part of human civilization since the earliest days of recorded history. The ancient Greeks used the word *phantasma* to describe a ghost. The ancient Romans referred to ghosts with the Latin word *spiritus*. The early French-speaking peoples used the term *spectre*. The peoples of the Nordic countries used the term *aptr-ganga*, meaning "back-comer."

The modern English word for *ghost* seems to have originated in Middle Europe. Inhabitants of the Germanic countries used such terms as *ghoizdos* and *gheest*—both of which mean spirit. The German term *gheis* means to be excited, amazed, or frightened. As language evolved in medieval England, people used the phrases *gæstan*, which means to frighten and *gast*, meaning soul or spirit. These words are likely to be at the root of the modern term *ghastly*, which is used to describe a person or entity that is horrible or frightening.

Ghastly also describes something or someone with a ghost-like appearance—in other words, an entity that is deathlike, pale, gruesome, or macabre. Says Leo Ruickbie, "Human history is the history of the non-human and the unreal. Throughout our recorded history—from rock carving to the Internet—the human race has made reference to another, radically different order of beings and alternatives to physical reality. . . . From our earliest myths to our latest fears, the supernatural has always been with us."[23]

> "From our earliest myths to our latest fears, the supernatural has always been with us."[23]
>
> —Historian Leo Ruickbie.

Inventing Myths

The fact that the various peoples of the world, speaking a variety of languages, needed to find words to describe ghosts indicates that people within those cultures harbored genuine beliefs in ghosts. The ancient world knew little about science or nature, which might explain why the citizens of ancient Greece believed in spirits. To explain natural occurrences—perhaps why it rained one day and not the next, or why disease took the lives of their loved ones, or why the stars shone at night—they invented myths.

Knowing little about meteorology—the science of the weather—the Greeks found it far easier to explain the sinking of a ship as being due to the wrath of the sea god Poseidon. After all, they knew nothing of how changes in air pressure in the atmosphere may spawn high winds that could mean peril to the

Lacking scientific explanations for natural phenomena, the ancient Greeks blamed these occurrences on supernatural beings, including Poseidon (pictured). As god of the oceans, Poseidon was thought to be responsible for events such as ships sinking during a storm at sea.

mariners of the era. Says Karen Armstrong, well-known writer on comparative religions,

> We are meaning-seeking creatures. Dogs, as far as we know, do not agonise about the canine condition, worry about the plight of dogs in other parts of the world, or try to see their lives from a different perspective. But human beings fall easily into despair, and from the very beginning we invented stories that enabled us to place our lives in a larger setting, that revealed an underlying pattern, and gave us a sense that, against all the depressing and chaotic evidence to the contrary, life had meaning and value.[24]

To Explain the Unexplainable

As the peoples of the ancient world concocted myths to explain the unexplainable, they also developed literature and the arts. As authors told their stories they often included mythical elements, including the existence of ghosts, in their works. In his epic poem the *Iliad*—which tells of the Greek siege of the city of Troy—ninth-century-BCE poet Homer wrote of the shade, or ghost, of Patroclus, the dead comrade of the hero Achilles. In the poem Patroclus visits Achilles as he sleeps. "You neglect me now I'm dead, as you never did when I was alive," Patroclus tells Achilles. "Hasten my funeral, and let me pass Hades' Gate. The spirits keep me out, the shades of men done with toil, who will not let me join them beyond the river, but leave me wandering in vain this side of the yawning Gate."[25]

The ancient Romans concocted a myth to explain how their city was founded in 753 BCE. The myth includes the appearance of a ghost. According to the story, the city was founded by twins, Romulus and Remus. When they were just babies, the brothers were tossed into the Tiber River. They were rescued by a shepherd, Faustulus, and suckled by a she-wolf. When the twins reached adulthood they became fierce warriors, and founded the city of Rome. After establishing their city the two brothers quar-

Ghosts of Ancient Greece

The ancient Greeks not only believed in ghosts but also established categories of ghosts. The *aoroi*, for example, were ghosts of people who died before fulfilling their potential in the mortal world. "Those cheated of their full stint of life bitterly stayed back to haunt the land of the living of which they had been deprived," says Daniel Ogden, a professor of ancient history at the University of Exeter in Great Britain. "In theory, anyone who died of anything other than natural causes in old age could generate a ghost."

Greeks also believed in the *biothanatoi*, ghosts of people who died through violent means. Victims of murder and suicide could become *biothanatoi*, but the category also included soldiers who died on the battlefield as well as criminals executed for their crimes.

The *agamoi* were ghosts of people who died before they had the opportunity to marry. Males and females could both become *agamoi*, but the category was believed to be dominated by the ghosts of bitter young women who missed out on the opportunities to become wives and mothers.

Finally, the Greeks believed in the *ataophoi*—ghosts whose bodies were denied burial—an important rite in the Greek world. These spirits could include sailors lost at sea and others whose bodies were never found. Says Ogden, "Whatever the circumstances of death, a ghost could not achieve rest without the due funeral rites."

Daniel Ogden, *Magic, Witchcraft and Ghosts in the Greek and Roman Worlds*. New York: Oxford University Press, 2009, p. 146.

reled over who should be king, with the quarrel ending in the slaying of Remus by his brother.

Roman legend holds that the ghost of Remus visited Faustulus and asked him to convince Romulus to name a holiday in his memory. Romulus agreed, and declared May 9 the *Lemuria*—or day of the ghosts. That legend spawned a ritual in ancient Rome known as the *Lemuralia* in which the head of a household cleansed his home of ghosts. The early-twentieth-century British scholar Lacy Collison-Morley describes the *Lemuralia*:

> The head of the family walked through the house with bare feet at dead of night, making the mystic sign with his first and fourth fingers extended, the other fingers being turned inwards and the thumb crossed over them, in case he might run against an unsubstantial spirit as he moved noiselessly along. . . .
>
> After solemnly washing his hands, he places black beans in his mouth, and throws others over his shoulders, saying, "With these beans do I redeem me and mine." He repeats this ceremony nine times without looking round, and the spirits are thought to follow unseen and pick up the beans. Then he purifies himself once more and clashes brass, and bids the demons leave his house. When . . . the ceremony is over [the] restless ghosts have been duly laid for a year.[26]

Spirits in Judaism and Buddhism

The peoples of ancient Greece and Rome, as well as other ancient cultures such as those in Egypt, Babylonia, and Phoenicia, were polytheistic, meaning they believed in many gods. Eventually many cultures established monotheistic religions—the belief in a single deity. As with the polytheistic faiths, many of these religions made room for ghost stories. Among the beliefs harbored in ancient Hebrew culture was the existence of the *ruhot*, or spirits, and the *mazzikim*, or destructive spirits. Moreover, the ancient Jews believed in the existence of the *dybbuk*—a wandering soul that can possess a living person, controlling the body and actions of the person to carry out the will of the *dybbuk*. In Hebrew the word *dybbuk* means to cling.

Eliezer ben Elijah Ashkenazi, a sixteenth-century Jewish scholar, explained how spirits taking over the body of the living could communicate through the voices of those they possessed: "The throat is an apt vessel to make the voice audible. . . . Thus the body will make its voice and its speech heard in that throat, without moving the lips at all. And people commonly say of the fallen that an evil spirit . . . has entered them."[27]

The belief in the *preta* is part of the Buddhist faith. The *preta* is also known as the hungry ghost and is portrayed as having a large and empty belly, thin neck, and small mouth. According to Buddhist teachings, the hungry ghost represents the human failings of greed, envy, and obsession. The *preta* will never know peace until it leaves its earthly desires behind.

Ghosts in the Scriptures

Ghost stories also appear in the Old Testament. In the First Book of Samuel, the beleaguered King Saul summons the Witch of Endor to call the dead Samuel from the grave to ask his advice in waging war against the Philistines: "Then Samuel said to Saul, 'Why have you disturbed me by bringing me up?' And Saul answered, 'I am greatly distressed; for the Philistines are waging war against me, and God has departed from me and no longer answers me, either through prophets or by dreams; therefore I have called you, that you may make known to me what I should do.'"[28]

And although Christianity does not recognize the existence of ghosts, there are still references to ghosts in the New Testament. The Gospel of Matthew states, "When the disciples saw Him walking on the sea, they were terrified, and said, 'It is a ghost!' And they cried out in fear."[29] According to the Gospel of Luke, when Christ appears to the apostles after the resurrection they believe they are witnessing a ghost. "But they were startled and frightened," Luke says, "and supposed that they saw a spirit." Jesus responds, "See my hands and my feet, that it is I myself; handle me, and see; for a spirit has not flesh and bones as you see that I have."[30]

Moreover, one of the earliest recorded stories involving a ghost was found in the writings of Pope Gregory I, who headed the Catholic Church in the sixth century. Gregory wrote about a priest who visited a hot spring to bathe. The priest encountered a polite and helpful stranger who assisted the priest in removing his garments and dressing after his bath. The priest assumed his helper to be a servant, and when he prepared to leave he offered to pay the man, but the man refused. The priest returned several more times, and each time the helper appeared and attended to the priest's needs—and each time refused payment. Finally, the priest arrived at the lake carrying two Eucharist loaves—loaves of bread that he blessed through a religious ritual—and offered them to his helper. According to Gregory,

> But then with a sad countenance the man said to the priest: "Why did you give me these, father? This is holy bread, and I cannot eat it. For I, whom you see here, was once the overseer of these baths, and am now after my death appointed for my sins to this place. But if you wish to please me, offer this bread unto Almighty God, and be an intercessor for my sins. And by this shall you know that your prayers have been heard, if when you come again you find me not here." And as he was speaking, he suddenly vanished; so that, although he previously seemed to be a man, he showed by his manner of departure that he was a spirit.[31]

According to Gregory, the priest carried out the ghost's wishes and prayed that his soul would find peace. The priest never saw the man—or ghost—again.

Renaissance Ghosts

Such reports of ghostly sightings were readily accepted by Europeans who were deeply religious and overwhelmingly Christian. By the Renaissance—the period of European history between the fourteenth and seventeenth centuries that saw great advances in art, literature, and science—the belief in ghosts was widely ingrained in European culture. Quite simply, people believed in ghosts and other paranormal phenomena such as witchcraft, alchemy, and existence of the devil. And so when the dramatists of the era staged new theatrical plays they found their audiences willing to accept the presence of ghosts without questioning their authenticity.

That was particularly true in the Elizabethan era—the period in English history from the mid-1500s to early 1600s when the country was ruled by Queen Elizabeth I. Indeed, William Shakespeare—the greatest dramatist in the history of the theater—filled his plays with ghosts as well as witches and other supernatural characters. Among Shakespeare's plays in which ghosts appear are *Julius Caesar*, *Macbeth*, *Richard III*, and *Hamlet*. In *Macbeth*, for example, the character Macbeth—who has murdered King Duncan of Scotland to attain the throne—also slays his friend and rival Banquo and is

This nineteenth-century painting depicts a scene from William Shakespeare's play Macbeth, *in which the ghost of Banquo appears. In Shakespeare's day, most Europeans believed in ghosts, witches, and other supernatural beings.*

thereafter haunted by the apparition of Banquo. Throughout the play the ghost of Banquo repeatedly appears on stage but is visible only to Macbeth. At one point, upon seeing the ghost of Banquo Macbeth cries out:

> . . . quit my sight! let the earth hide thee!
> Thy bones are marrowless, thy blood is cold;
> Thou hast no speculation in those eyes
> Which thou dost glare with![32]

As far as Shakespeare's audiences were concerned, ghosts were real and played genuine roles in the real-life tragedies that Shakespeare often dramatized. In *Julius Caesar*, for example, the ghost of the slain dictator appears to his assassin, Brutus, which Brutus interprets as an omen that his war against the Roman army has been lost. Brutus accepts his fate and falls on his sword. Says Shakespearean scholar Howard Waters:

> Where witches and ghosts were concerned, it was commonly accepted that they existed and the person who scoffed at them was considered foolish, or even likely to be cursed. . . .
>
> Ghosts were recognized by the Elizabethans in three basic varieties: the vision or purely subjective ghost, the authentic ghost who has died without opportunity of repentance, and the false ghost which is capable of many types of manifestations. . . .
>
> Shakespeare's audiences, and his plays, were the products of their culture. Since the validity of any literary work can best be judged by its public acceptance, not to mention its lasting power, it seems that Shakespeare's ghosts and witches were, and are, enormously popular. If modern audiences and critics find themselves a bit skeptical, then they might consider bringing along a . . . willing suspension of disbelief. Elizabethans simply had no need of it.[33]

Scary Classics

After Shakespeare's era the public's thirst for ghost stories never seemed to be quenched. Many of the greatest writers in history have produced ghost stories. In 1820 American writer Washington Irving published a classic short story, "The Legend of Sleepy Hollow," in which dastardly schoolmaster Ichabod Crane finds himself chased by the ghostly Headless Horseman. British writer Charles Dickens, known for such classics as *David Copperfield*, *Oliver Twist*, and *A Tale of Two Cities*, is also the author of *A Christmas Carol*, which he published in 1843. Much more than a story celebrating a joyous holiday, *A Christmas Carol* follows the miserly protagonist Ebenezer Scrooge as he is led on a mystical journey by ghostly guides.

In the same year *A Christmas Carol* was published, American author Edgar Allan Poe published the short story "A Tell-Tale Heart," in which the thumping heart of a murder victim terrorizes his killer. Mark Twain had fun with ghosts in his 1875 short story "A Ghost Story," but not much fun was found in British author Henry James's 1898 scary classic *The Turn of the Screw*, in which a governess discovers the eerie connection between two ghosts and the children under her watch. And starting in 2001 British writer J.K. Rowling's enormously popular books about boy sorcerer Harry Potter all feature visits by ghosts.

> "Where witches and ghosts were concerned, it was commonly accepted that they existed and the person who scoffed at them was considered foolish, or even likely to be cursed."[33]
>
> —*Shakespearean scholar Howard Waters.*

Ghosts on the Air

By the twentieth century the movie industry had blossomed, and filmmakers found audiences craving stories about ghosts. These movies include the 1937 comedy *Topper* in which a fun-loving wealthy couple returns from the dead to playfully haunt their eternally glum friend. An even more comedic look at ghosts can be found in the 1983 film *Ghostbusters*, in which a team of clumsy paranormal investigators is enlisted to save the city of New York from a plague of ghosts. A touching story could be found in the

1990 film *Ghost*, a romance in which a man returns from the dead to comfort his grief-stricken wife.

But for the most part, ghost films have been horror films, intended to frighten their audiences. *The Haunting*, released in 1963 and based on a story by American author Shirley Jackson, focuses on a group of paranormal investigators as they spend a night in a haunted house. In more recent years, such films as *Ouija*, *Annabelle*, *The Conjuring*, *R.I.P.D.*, *Paranormal Activity*, and the film adaptations of the Harry Potter books focus on ghostly activities.

A poster advertises the 2012 movie Paranormal Activity 4. *Like many recent films, those in the hugely popular* Paranormal Activity *series revolve around ghostly occurrences. Tales about the supernatural have also regularly appeared on television since the medium became widely available in the 1950s.*

TV has also featured series with paranormal themes. Since the 1950s, when television became widely available to large audiences, TV producers have filled their viewers' desire to see ghost stories. Among the series that regularly featured ghost stories are *One Step Beyond* and *Twilight Zone* in the 1950s; *Night Gallery* and *The Ghost and Mrs. Muir* in the 1960s; *Kolchak: The Night Stalker* in the 1970s; *Tales from the Darkside* in the 1980s; *Goosebumps* and *X-Files* in the 1990s, and *Ghost Whisperer* and *Supernatural* in the 2000s.

These TV series and others were all fictionalized accounts of ghostly encounters, but with the growing popularity of reality TV many paranormal investigators have been enlisted by TV producers to film their own ghost hunts. Numerous paranormal-themed reality shows air on cable TV, among them *The Haunted*, *Haunted History*, *Ghost Adventures*, *Ghost Hunters*, *Ghostly Encounters*, *Paranormal State*, and *The Unexplained*.

> "Although many who read these books and watch these movies and television shows may not take them as reflections of the real world, it is safe to assume that many others do."[34]
>
> —*Psychology professor Stuart Vyse.*

Dealing with Grief

With ghost stories so much a part of popular culture it is not surprising that many people believe in the existence of ghosts. Says Stuart Vyse, a psychology professor at Connecticut College and an expert on superstition, "Although many who read these books and watch these movies and television shows may not take them as reflections of the real world, it is safe to assume that many others do."[34]

Experts suggest that people believe in ghosts in the twenty-first century for the same reason they believed in ghosts in the era of the ancient Greeks: Supernatural phenomena help them understand things they find no other way to explain. Says Christopher French, a professor of psychology at the University of London, "What we have is people trying to make sense of something that, to them, seems inexplicable. So you get the misinterpretation of noises or visual effects that do have a normal explanation, but not one that people can think of. People assume that if they cannot explain something in natural terms, then it must be something paranormal."[35]

Some people may harbor beliefs in ghosts as a way of convincing themselves that they wield a measure of control over events they cannot control. Adam Waytz, a professor at Northwestern University in Evanston, Illinois, uses the example of a tree limb tapping against a window: Some people may look upon the tapping noise as a ghost trying to send them a message. "We create beliefs in ghosts, because we don't like believing that the universe is random,"[36] he says. Benjamin Radford, managing editor of the science magazine *Skeptical Inquirer*, says many people believe in ghosts as a way of dealing with their grief over the loss of family members. He says, "The idea that the dead remain with us in spirit is an ancient one, and one that offers many people comfort; who doesn't want to believe that our beloved but deceased family members aren't looking out for us, or with us in our times of need? Most people believe in ghosts because of personal experience; they have seen or sensed some unexplained presence."[37]

> "The idea that the dead remain with us in spirit is an ancient one, and one that offers many people comfort; who doesn't want to believe that our beloved but deceased family members aren't looking out for us, or with us in our times of need?"[37]
>
> —Skeptical Inquirer editor Benjamin Radford.

Accepting Fable as Fact

Another reason for a belief in ghosts is that many people are simply gullible—they tend to believe what they are told. If they have been told at some point in their lives that a creepy-looking mansion in their town is haunted, they may accept the fable as fact. That was the conclusion drawn by a group of psychologists who published a study in 2011. Among the cases cited in the study was a 2005 incident at Mayland State University. The incident occurred at the university's Wozler Science Center, which had been constructed in 1890 and had, for decades, been rumored to be haunted. On March 12, 2005, four students

History of the Headless Horseman

First published in 1820, "The Legend of Sleepy Hollow" is regarded as America's first ghost story. Written by Washington Irving, the story is set in 1790 in Tarrytown, New York. The story recounts the haunting of schoolmaster Ichabod Crane who is chased on horseback by a ghost lacking a head. The ghost is a dead Hessian soldier—a German mercenary who fought on the side of the British in the American Revolution—who lost his head to a cannonball.

In creating the story of a headless horseman, Irving may have been influenced by legends he came across during his travels through Europe. In 1505 a German clergyman, Geiler von Kaysersberg, delivered a sermon in which he warned his flock of headless ghosts riding atop horses during an event he called the Wild Hunt. Also, the German poet Gottfried August Bürger published a poem in 1796, *"Der Wilde Jäger"* ("The Wild Hunstman"), which features a headless horseman.

Brian Haughton is an archaeologist who studies the influences of supernatural folklore. He says that in the era in which Irving's story was published many readers were willing to accept ghosts as fact. According to Haughton, "The Legend of Sleepy Hollow" shaped many people's ideas about the nature of ghosts: scary, evil, and dangerous. He says, "Irving's dark story of the headless Hessian soldier who rides forth every night through the dark lanes of Sleepy Hollow, and the [conclusion] of the tale involving a supernatural wild chase through the woods, has had a significant effect on the nature of American hauntings."

Brian Haughton, *Lore of the Ghost: The Origins of the Most Famous Ghost Stories Throughout the World*. Franklin Lakes, NJ: Career Press, 2008, p. 57.

were working in a lab in the building when they reported hearing noises and voices from the lab next door—even though that lab was closed for the evening. The students alerted campus police, but when officers investigated they found the lab locked and empty.

As for the students, the only explanation they could offer was a visit by ghosts. "I heard bangs and shuffling in the lab next to ours, and then I heard voices followed by more bangs," said sophomore Miles Layforth. "The lights were off and the door was locked in that lab. I have never experienced anything like that in my life. The experience changed my beliefs regarding the supernatural." And junior Susan Telesca said, "We were frightened by the noises. No natural explanations exist for what occurred. We all heard the voices and noises. It was a surreal experience."[38]

Blurred Lines

The authors of the study concluded that the students decided the lab was haunted because they chose to believe the old rumors about the haunted science building. These students were not unlike the people of ancient Rome who practiced the ritual of the *Lemuralia*, the Hebrews who believed in the *ruhot* and the *mazzikim*, the audiences for Shakespeare's plays who found no reason to question the authenticity of Banquo's ghost, or the fans of *Twilight Zone* or *Ghost Hunters*. For these people and others, the line between fiction and reality has always been blurred. They find no reason to suspend their disbelief.

Chapter 3

Searching for Ghosts

"I have been an active paranormal investigator for more than a decade, and in that time I've visited hundreds of haunted locations and interviewed thousands of people. Using scientific data gathering . . . I've come to understand spiritual activity on a realistic scale."

—Paranormal investigator Joshua P. Warren.

Joshua P. Warren, *How to Hunt Ghosts: A Practical Guide*. New York: Fireside, 2003, p. xi.

"I don't think you'll ever get me to believe in ghosts unless you show me a repeatable set of circumstances in which documented ghosts appear. . . . Coming from a really hard-headed 'you've got to show me' type such as myself, that amounts to a serious conversion."

—James D. Stein, professor of mathematics, California State University at Long Beach.

James D. Stein, *The Paranormal Equation: A New Scientific Perspective on Remote Viewing, Clairvoyance, and Other Inexplicable Phenomena*. Pompton Plains, NJ: New Page, 2013, p. 39.

In 1882 a group of British college professors, mathematicians, scientists, and other scholars established the first organization dedicated to the study of ghosts and other paranormal phenomena. The Society for Psychical Research dedicated itself to a sincere study of the supernatural. It had two goals: to root out phony mediums and other perpetrators of hoaxes and to determine whether scientific techniques could be applied to the search for spirits.

One of the founding members of the society was Frederic W.H. Myers, a poet and professor of classical literature.

Myers, who died in 1901, spent many years working on a scientific study of paranormal phenomena. In his seven-hundred-page book *Human Personality and Its Survival of Bodily Death*, Myers points out that for years people had attempted to communicate with the spirits of the dead through mediums, but it was now time to take a scientific approach to the topic. He writes,

> The question for man most momentous of all is whether or no he has an immortal soul; or—to avoid the word *immortal*, which belongs to the realm of infinities—whether or no his personality involves any element which can survive bodily death. In this direction have always lain the gravest fears, the farthest-reaching hopes, which could either oppress or stimulate mortal minds.
>
> On the other hand, the method which our race has found most effective in acquiring knowledge is by this time familiar to all men. It is the method of modern Science.[39]

Few Scientific Tools

In reality, though, Myers and his colleagues did not have many scientifically based tools with which to pursue their explorations of the paranormal. In the late nineteenth and early twentieth centuries photography was still in its infancy. Audio recording was in its infancy as well. The equipment to record voices and other sounds was large, cumbersome, and ill suited for use in cemeteries or other remote places that ghosts were likely to haunt. Mostly the well-intentioned members of the committee read through newspaper stories and other published sources to determine whether reports of ghost sightings had any measure of validity. They also attended séances, deciding for themselves whether the mediums were frauds.

And despite their dedication to using science to determine the validity of paranormal phenomena, in many cases society members found the mediums to be true communicators with the spirit world. In one case, for example, Myers reported on the investigation of a medium identified as Mrs. Piper, writing, "The medium has been under observation, much of the time under close observation . . . by a large number of persons, eager, many of them, to pounce upon any suspicious circumstance for [nearly] fifteen years. During that time . . . there [has] not been one single suspicious circumstance remarked."[40]

Electromagnetism and Spirits

In the modern era the desire to prove the existence of spirits through the use of scientific methods is as avid as it was a century ago. But unlike the founding members of the Society for Psychical Research, today's ghost hunters have access to a variety of scientific instruments with which to pursue evidence of the spirit world.

One tool employed by ghost hunters is the electromagnetic field (EMF) meter. The meters are used by electricians and electrical utility workers to determine whether heavy cables that conduct electricity are working properly. If the flow of electricity recedes or

The owner of a Florida ghost-hunting store poses with an electromagnetic field (EMF) meter. Commonly used by utility workers to determine whether electrical cables are working properly, EMF meters are also used by paranormal researchers, who believe ghosts emit electromagnetism.

surges through the line, there could be a problem—perhaps a break in the line or defective equipment that emits too much or too little electricity. If the line is experiencing problems, then fluctuations in the electromagnetic field, which is an invisible force of nature, are often emitted from the cable. The EMF meter, held close to the cable, provides information on the strength of the electromagnetic field.

Ghost hunters believe spirits of the dead emit electromagnetism, and that is why the hunters carry EMF meters on their investigations. Ghost hunters Jason Hawes and Grant Wilson contend that in 2000 they found evidence of a poltergeist at a Skowhegan, Maine, farmhouse, thanks to the EMF meters they carried during the investigation.

Temperature Changes

Hawes, Wilson, and three other members of their team had been called to the farmhouse by the owners, Gary and Diane Eshelmann. The couple had been hearing strange noises in their home. At times the Eshelmanns and their children felt themselves mysteriously shoved from behind. Their son Robert's skin showed unexplainable scratches. Family members also reported seeing objects flying across the rooms of the home. "Right from the beginning we began to get a sense of what the family had been going through," says Hawes. "Doors slammed in our faces, without any rational explanation. A couple of our investigators felt something hot against their skin and, moments later, found scratches there. There was growling coming from somewhere in the house, though we couldn't figure out where."[41]

The team spread out and searched for the poltergeist. Throughout the night they heard weird noises—some sounding as though they were made by animals, some evidently the screams of the ghost. In addition to their EMF meters, the team members were equipped with highly sensitive thermometers that can detect the slightest drops in temperature. When a ghost enters a room it is believed to attract the energy in the room, thus reducing the temperature. "We experienced one temperature change after another, all throughout the house," says Hawes. "First we would record sixty-eight degrees, then it would rise to ninety degrees, and afterward it would plummet to forty degrees. The changes were drastic, and therefore unlikely to have natural causes."[42]

Other evidence soon surfaced: A foul odor resembling sulfur invaded their noses. Some investigators saw orbs. The investigators heard shouts of "Get out!" and "Come to hell!" And then they looked at their EMF meters. "Our EMF meters were jumping all over the place," says Hawes. "There was no natural explanation for the activity, as far as we could tell."[43] Eventually the ghostly activity in the Eshelmann house ceased—which is typical of poltergeists. Ghost hunters tell their clients that poltergeists have their fun and then move on to haunt somewhere else. As for Hawes and Wilson, they have no doubts the Maine farmhouse was visited by a poltergeist.

But others are not so sure. Benjamin Radford says scientific instruments such as EMF detectors and thermometers cannot measure what is simply not there—a paranormal entity. He says,

> Virtually all ghost hunter groups claim to be scientific, and most give that appearance because they use high-tech scientific equipment. . . . Yet the equipment is only as scientific as the person using it; you may own the world's most sophisticated thermometer, but if you are using it as a barometer, your measurements are worthless. Just as using a calculator doesn't make you a mathematician, using a scientific instrument doesn't make you a scientist.[44]

Spinning Compass Needles

Another device employed by modern ghost hunters is the Gauss multidetector, which measures magnetism. Ghosts are believed to upset magnetic fields—the presence of a ghost, for example, would make a compass needle spin in circles. (The instrument draws its name from the nineteenth-century German mathematician Carl Friedrich Gauss, whose work helped establish the scientific principles of magnetism.)

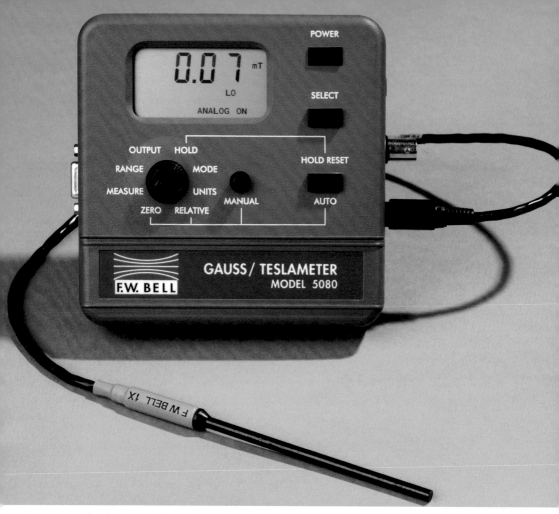

The Gauss multidetector, which measures magnetism, is a tool used by paranormal researchers. Since ghosts are believed to alter magnetic fields, any unusual activity the instrument detects might indicate that a spirit is nearby.

Paranormal investigators use the Gauss multidetector to determine the validity of ectoplasm—a gooey, milky white substance left behind by a ghost. Reports also suggest that ectoplasm can appear in a misty, fog-like substance. The term has its roots in the Greek words *ekto* and *plasma*, meaning exteriorized substance. In some cases the ectoplasm merely leaks out as an ooze, but people who claim to have seen ectoplasm report that it had taken shape. Many reports of ectoplasm suggest the substance forms itself into the head of the ghost, or the ghost's hands, or some other hideous manifestation such as tentacles.

Such a manifestation of ectoplasm was recorded in 2007 by Kenneth Harmon of Fort Collins, Colorado. After moving into their home, Harmon; his wife, Monika; and daughters Sarah, Michelle, Amanda, and Rebecca started seeing evidence of a ghost. First, their poodle Rosie exhibited strange behavior—cowering and hiding beneath a bed for no apparent reason. Photographs taken inside the home indicated the presence of orbs as well as faint, gray outlines of what appeared to be a human figure. Moreover, the posture of the figure changed from photo to photo, indicating that the spirit was in motion. In the photos Harmon discovered a greenish cloud hovering near a window; some photos showed the cloud forming into eerie shapes. Says Harmon, "A cluster of spheres appears above Michelle's head as she stands near the sliding door in the kitchen. When you zoom in on one of them near the top of the group, you can see a face."[45] Harmon believes the cloud was composed of ectoplasm.

> "A cluster of spheres appears above Michelle's head as she stands near the sliding door in the kitchen. When you zoom in on one of them near the top of the group, you can see a face."[45]
>
> —Kenneth Harmon, who recorded a manifestation of ectoplasm.

Disrupting Magnetism

In 2008 a team of paranormal investigators in Jackson County, Florida, claimed to detect evidence of ectoplasm in an old house where haunting activity had been reported. The residence, known as the Russ House, had been the home of a prominent citizen of Jackson County, Joseph W. Russ. Russ had committed suicide in the house in 1930.

Betty Davis, the founder of Big Bend Ghost Trackers, the organization that discovered the ectoplasm, used a Gauss multidetector in searching for the ghost. According to Davis, the device registered medium to high readings, indicating a disruption in the magnetism of a room where members of the team reported seeing ectoplasm floating in the air. "[It was] a misty, slightly foggy substance . . . residue left over by a spirit who was recently in an area,"[46] says Davis.

Skeptics insist, though, that there is no scientific basis for the existence of ectoplasm. Says Robert Todd Carroll, author of *The*

Skeptic's Dictionary and former professor of philosophy at Sacramento City College in California,

> Ectoplasm is stuff that allegedly oozes from ghosts or spirits. . . . In the heyday of séances—the 19th and early 20th centuries—ectoplasm oozed from various orifices of mediums. . . .
>
> A bit of white cloth-like (very cloth-like) material oozing from someone's mouth, ears, or nose was considered strong evidence for the afterlife by those who think spirits are not dwelling in Heaven or Hell or some other distant gated community but are floating around the earth trying to give us material hints of their existence. Most photographs of ectoplasm make it look like the kind of stuff you could pick up at the local [fabric] store or buy from Amazon.[47]

Electronic Voice Phenomena

Although paranormal investigators believe Gauss multidetectors, EMF meters, and similar devices can capture evidence of spirits, skeptics such as Carroll and Radford insist the data these devices collect is open to interpretation. Indeed, such skeptics argue that evidence of fluctuations in electromagnetism or temperature in a particular area does not mean a ghost is in the neighborhood. That is why paranormal investigators place most of their trust in devices that are able to capture the sounds made by ghosts, as well as cameras that are able to capture the actual images of spirits.

While voice recording equipment dates back to Myers's era, ghost hunters believe the ability to record the voices of the dead took a great step forward in the 1960s when handheld cassette tape recorders became available and, more recently, with the development of digital voice recorders. These devices are mobile and

"Most photographs of ectoplasm make it look like the kind of stuff you could pick up at the local [fabric] store or buy from Amazon."[47]

—Robert Todd Carroll, author of The Skeptic's Dictionary.

New Tools for Ghost Hunters

Gauss multidetectors and sensitive thermometers are important tools for paranormal investigators, but many ghost hunters rely on even more sophisticated equipment. Among those tools are digital thermal hygrometers, used by meteorologists to measure humidity. Hygrometers are helpful in ruling out false evidence of orbs. In humid conditions airborne water vapor may cause white spots to appear on digital images, and these spots can be misinterpreted as orbs. If the paranormal investigator uses a hygrometer while taking the picture and determines the humidity levels are low at that time, humidity can be ruled out as a reason for the appearance of the orbs in the photograph.

Another new tool employed by ghost hunters is an ion detector. Ions are atoms that emit electrical charges because of imbalances in their protons and electrons. Physicists use ion detectors to determine the radioactivity of elements. In theory, when a ghost enters an area it absorbs energy, causing an increase in ion emissions. Therefore, the ion detector is helpful in detecting the presence of a ghost. "It is a fascinating tool in the paranormal investigator's arsenal," says ghost hunter Melissa Martin Ellis.

Sound level meters are helpful in recording the voices of ghosts. The meters do not actually record sounds but instead detect noises that may be imperceptible to the human ear. Therefore, the meters can help find the quietest places in a haunted location to listen for ghosts, meaning unwanted noises that may garble the voice of a spirit would not be recorded.

Melissa Martin Ellis, *The Everything Ghost Hunting Book: Tips, Tools, and Techniques for Exploring the Supernatural World*. Avon, MA: Adams Media, 2014, p. 123.

can therefore be used to follow the trail of a ghost. "Recorders are small devices that pack lots of investigative punch and can be extremely useful and inexpensive investigative tools," says paranormal investigator Melissa Martin Ellis. "In fact, they are so indispensable and affordable that they are recommended as an essential part of any paranormal toolkit."[48] To paranormal investigators the voice of a spirit captured on tape or through digital recording is known as electronic voice phenomena, or EVP.

A Soldier's Voice

Paranormal investigators Patrick Burke and Jack Roth have visited Gettysburg, Pennsylvania, many times over the years, hoping to acquire evidence of the existence of ghosts of the soldiers who died at the Battle of Gettysburg during the Civil War. On May 7, 2004, members of a team of investigators led by Burke and Roth believe they captured the voice of a fallen soldier.

The recording occurred at Spangler's Spring, a stream that flows through the battlefield. Members of the paranormal investigating team fanned out along the stream banks, each carrying microcassette tape recorders. Explain Burke and Roth:

> We asked a particular field investigator named Heather to take her microcassette recorder and sit on a rock by the actual spring. Once there, she performed an EVP experiment during which she asked certain questions in twenty-second intervals, thus providing enough time for a possible response. Upon playback of her tape, she ran to us in a rather excited state and suggested she may have captured something. When we listened to the recording, we all heard the following very clearly at the midpoint of her questioning:
>
> Heather: Do you like it here?
>
> Voice (male—low but clearly audible): Hell no![49]

Burke and Roth believe Heather successfully recorded the voice of a spirit. Strangely, two weeks after Heather recorded the voice it disappeared from the tape. "At first we thought she must have erased it, but she was adamant about being careful with it," Burke and Roth report. According to the paranormal investigators, it is not unusual for the voices of spirits to erase themselves from electronic recording equipment. "EVP is a promising, yet frustrating area of study within the world of paranormal research,"[50] concede Burke and Roth.

Photographic Evidence

Ghosts may be able to wipe evidence of their existence from voice recorders, but paranormal investigators find they have more success in maintaining photographic records of the spirit world. Investigators have collected many still photographs—both on film and digitally—as well as video footage of apparitions. "A picture is worth a thousand words," says Ellis. "That's never been truer than when it is applied to pictures of the paranormal. . . . It is still truly stunning to see video or still photos of apparitions or ghosts."[51]

One of the most famous images of a ghost is believed to be included in a portrait of the crew of the HMS *Daedalus*, a ship of the British navy that sailed nearly a century ago. The 1919 portrait of the crew displays more than fifty sailors and officers. But there is an extra face among the crew members—the face of Freddy Jackson, who died in an accident two days before the photo was taken.

Another noted photograph of an apparent ghost depicts Lady Townshend, a British noblewoman who died in 1726 while confined by her husband, the Duke of Monmouth, to her family's mansion, known as Raynham Hall. The image, photographed in 1936, depicts an apparition of Lady Townshend, known as the Brown Lady, as she glides down a flight of stairs.

The photograph was taken by Hubert C. Provand, a photographer working for *Country Life*, a magazine that planned to publish a feature story on the mansion. The ghost was first observed by Provand's assistant, Indre Shira, who shouted, "There's something on the steps!"[52] Provand aimed the camera but did not see the apparition. "There's not a bloody thing there,"[53] he responded. Still, Provand fired the shutter. Provand did not believe he caught anything unusual on film, but after developing the photo he discovered that he had captured the translucent, smoky image of the Brown Lady. Later, the photograph of the Brown Lady appeared in a 1937 issue of *Life*, a widely circulated magazine in America.

Ghosts on the Web

The science of photography has taken great leaps forward since the days when the Brown Lady and the crew of the HMS *Daedalus* were preserved on film. Now, in the digital age, photography has given ghost hunters highly sophisticated tools to capture images of apparitions.

Indeed, with the growth of the Internet, ghost hunters have found a new technique to detect paranormal activity: the webcam. In many places that are believed to be haunted, webcams

Modern technology enables ghost hunters to monitor a potentially haunted site from miles away using a webcam and a smartphone. Some websites provide links to active webcams that allow site visitors to view such scenes.

have been set up to monitor paranormal activity. In this way a ghost hunter can keep an eye on the haunted scene, miles away from the ghost, using a home computer or even smartphone. Says paranormal investigator Ryan Dube,

> [You] know how ghost hunting basically works. A team of researchers pack up two or three vans full of electronic recording equipment, haul it all to an allegedly haunted house, they'll then set up the equipment in every room, and then they'll sit in the dark all night waiting for something to happen. Half the time, they don't capture a single piece of evidence. This is not the way ghost hunting is supposed to work. Instead of going to the ghosts, use the Internet to let the ghosts come to you.[54]

Moreover, anybody with Internet access can now look for ghosts because several paranormal societies as well as individual ghost hunters have established websites with links to active webcams. One such site was established by the ghost-hunting group Louisiana Spirits Paranormal Investigations. By accessing the site, visitors can view links to several webcams.

One ghost believed to have made many appearances on a webcam is the spirit of a woman who is believed to have haunted the Willard Library in Evansville, Indiana, since 1937. Members of the library staff as well as library members have for years reported cold spots and an unusual scent of perfume throughout the library. Moreover, many staff members and library visitors—including two police officers answering a burglar alarm at the library—have reported actually seeing the apparition. They have described the ghost as a young woman dressed in gray with a veil covering her face. In 1999 a local newspaper, the *Evansville Courier & Press*, installed a webcam in the library that posts pictures on the Internet every thirty seconds. The spirit has been caught several times on the webcam. Images have shown the apparition walking up steps, sitting at tables, and pausing in front of shelves of books. "I think something is out there. . . . We stand

No Pay for Ghost Hunters

Anybody who desires to enter the field of paranormal investigations should know that they would not be able to make a living hunting for ghosts. The phony mediums of a century ago charged grieving relatives large sums to contact their deceased loved ones. Today's paranormal investigators believe their work would be questioned if they billed their haunted clients for their services. "Perhaps the biggest reason most contemporary investigators do not accept payment goes back to credibility issues," says paranormal investigator Deonna Kelli Sayed. "There is unfortunately a history of some who conducted ghost work exploiting desperate or frightened clients. Fraudulent mediums . . . set an unfortunate standard for those who travel in the ghost frontier."

But while modern ghost hunters are expected to perform their paranormal investigations without charge, they also need to obtain expensive scientific instruments to perform their probes into the paranormal. Gauss multidetectors, electromagnetic field meters, night vision goggles, digital cameras, videography equipment, digital voice recorders, and other instruments can cost several thousand dollars. There is also the cost of travel in the event the investigation must be conducted far from home. That is why Sayed urges paranormal investigators to form teams so they can share the cost of the equipment and travel. Even by forming teams, though, Sayed suggests team members should expect to shoulder at least $500 a year in expenses. "Ghost hunting is not cheap," she cautions.

Deonna Kelli Sayed, *So You Want to Hunt Ghosts? A Down to Earth Guide*. Woodbury, MN: Llewellyn, 2012, pp. 73, 82.

ready and willing to believe,"[55] says James Derk, director of new media for the *Courier & Press*.

Proving the Existence of Ghosts

Still, some experts remain skeptical. Even the paranormal society Angels & Ghosts cautions home-based ghost hunters to be wary of what they see on a webcam. According to the organization, such images are often blurry and therefore unreliable. Says the group, "By providing a live video feed of a certain haunted area, spectators can sit and watch as the web camera refreshes itself periodically, showing a new image each time. Though the image may appear the same as the one previously seen, some will notice subtle differences. These differences can be caused by technical and natural interferences."[56]

> "I think something is out there. . . . We stand ready and willing to believe."[55]
>
> —*James Derk, director of new media for the Courier & Press.*

Ghost hunters argue, though, that their techniques have come a long way since the members of the Society for Psychical Research could do little but pass judgment on what they read about ghost sightings in the newspapers. Today, paranormal investigators insist their probes of the spirit world are based on sound science—and they believe they have the electromagnetic readings, voice recordings, and webcam images to prove it.

Chapter 4

Are There Other Explanations for Ghosts?

"Evidence for ghosts seems to be getting worse, not better, in large part due to pranksters and ghost-generating apps. Several smartphone apps allow their users to easily tweak photos to make them look strange or mysterious, adding quasi-transparent ghostly images in the background."

—*Skeptical Inquirer* editor Benjamin Radford.

Benjamin Radford, "Fake Ghost Photos Haunt Real Ghost Researchers," LiveScience, November 15, 2011. www.livescience.com.

"Ghosts cannot be trapped in the laboratory. If you drag them out of the shadows and expose them to the harsh glare of scientific reality, they tend to vanish. Thanks to this science tells us ghosts cannot exist."

—Paranormal investigator Troy Taylor.

Troy Taylor, *The Ghost Hunter's Guidebook: The Common Sense Guide to Paranormal Research*. Chicago: Whitechapel, 2010, eBook.

Harry Houdini died in 1926, but Houdini's death did not bring an end to the campaign to unmask paranormal hoaxes. Scientists and others have for decades turned a skeptical eye toward reports of ghost sightings. They insist there are simple explanations for what people perceive as visits from the spirits of the dead.

Foremost among the explanations for ghostly phenomena is the idea that they are simply hoaxes—that some people today are as dedicated to fooling others into believing in the existence of ghosts as they were in Houdini's day. Says Benjamin Radford,

> If ghosts are real, and are some sort of as-yet-unknown energy or entity, then their existence will (like all other scientific discoveries) be verified by scientists through controlled experiments—not by weekend ghost hunters wandering around abandoned houses in the dark late at night with cameras and flashlights. In the end (and despite mountains of ambiguous photos, sounds and videos), the evidence for ghosts is no better today than it was a year ago, a decade ago or a century ago.[57]

But paranormal investigators insist that science has been unable to answer some questions about the spirit world. "Science always tries to label everything, and it has done a hell of a job," says Grant Wilson. "But sometimes the label it puts on something is inaccurate. Sometimes the answer falls outside the realm of established scientific knowledge."[58]

Mumler's Portrait of Mary Lincoln

As Radford states, images of ghosts have appeared in photographs for about as long as there have been cameras. In 1860 a New Jersey man named Campbell is believed to have made the first photograph of what he interpreted to be a ghost. Campbell is said to have photographed an empty chair, but when he developed the photo it showed an image of a young boy sitting in the chair. Since that day perhaps thousands of images of ghosts have appeared in photographs. One of the most famous of these was

"Science always tries to label everything, and it has done a hell of a job. But sometimes the label it puts on something is inaccurate. Sometimes the answer falls outside the realm of established scientific knowledge."[58]

—Paranormal investigator Grant Wilson.

Mary Todd Lincoln (pictured), widow of President Abraham Lincoln, was the subject of a doctored photograph supposedly showing the ghost of her deceased husband standing behind her. Today, technology has made it easier than ever before to produce this kind of fake but ghostly image.

taken sometime in the 1870s by Bostonian William Mumler. It was a portrait of Mary Todd Lincoln—herself a firm believer in the spirit world. In the portrait the apparition of her assassinated husband, President Lincoln, hovers behind the widow, even placing his hand on her shoulder.

Before photographing the portrait of Mrs. Lincoln, Mumler had made a career of taking photographs of ghosts. He took these jobs at the request of grieving families who sought images of their deceased loved ones. Authorities were skeptical, though, and charged him with defrauding his clients. During his 1869 trial, photography experts explained his very simple technique: double exposure. In the era of film photography, a crafty photographer simply used the same piece of film (or, in those days, a photographic plate similar to film) to photograph two different subjects. By varying the exposure—the amount of time the shutter is open—and by using techniques in the darkroom, the photographer could easily insert an apparition into the final image.

Mumler was acquitted. Many of his clients testified for the defense, insisting that Mumler helped ease their grief over the losses of their loved ones. This testimony evidently helped sway sympathetic jurors in his favor. After the trial he continued his photography career, photographing Mrs. Lincoln a short time later. But he did not fool anybody—except perhaps Mrs. Lincoln. Although by the 1870s the dead president was not available to sit for a portrait, there were plenty of photos of Lincoln that Mumler could re-photograph—take a picture of a picture—then double-expose that negative with the portrait he took of the president's widow. "William Mumler made a good living in Boston using double exposure to produce photographs with alleged spirits of dead people in them," says Robert Todd Carroll. "Many have followed in Mumler's footsteps."[59]

How to Fake a Ghost

Indeed, since Mumler's day anybody with a camera and darkroom skills could produce a ghostly image on film, and in the ensuing decades thousands of such images have surfaced. But now that film is used much less and digital photography is the state of the art, virtually anybody with a camera or smartphone and simple photo editing skills can make their photos as creepy as they desire. In fact, the Ghost Research Society, based in Oak Lawn, Illinois, cites more than twenty methods by which fake ghosts can be inserted into photos—both in film and in digital photography.

One method is to use long exposure: The photographer places the camera on a tripod and then opens the shutter for an exposure of ten or twenty seconds. That gives another person, masquerading as a spirit, enough time to run in front of the camera, pose for a second or two, and then dash out of the frame. The photo would then include a ghostly image of that person.

Many photographers who believe they have captured paranormal phenomena in their pictures may simply be in need of photography lessons. For example, photographers who claim to have found orbs on their digital images may have underexposed their subject. In other words, they opened and closed the shutter too quickly. In digital photography such an error often leads to orb-like white spots because the camera is not providing enough time for the colors of the image to fully reproduce.

And some photographers may believe they have captured the image of a ghost when all they have really done is let their camera strap get in the way of the lens when the shutter snaps. Since the strap is out of focus, it could be mistaken for a ghostly apparition. Says Dale Kaczmarek, president of the Ghost Research Society, "An object obstructing the lens causes a dark or black area. . . . Many so-called vortexes, swirls [and] spirals . . . are simply caused by . . . straps which are not around the picture-taker's neck but hanging loose. They then are captured in between the camera's lens and the subject of the photograph."[60]

Ghosts Aboard the SS *Watertown*

Still, Kaczmarek's group has chronicled many photographs of ghosts that are not as easy to explain as a long exposure trick or wayward camera strap. One picture in the society's collection was shot in 1979 with a Kodak 110 Instamatic camera—a very simple and inexpensive camera manufactured for amateur photographers. In other words, the camera did not possess the mechanical capabilities to permit the photographer much opportunity to pursue trick photography. The photo depicts a case of vandalism at a cemetery in Forest Park, Illinois. In the photo, the camera caught a streak of white light across a grassy field, and within the streak the face of a man is evident. Moreover, the

Painting with Light

One technique pranksters can use to give their photographs an eerie, ghostlike quality is known as painting with light. The procedure has been used for decades by photographers who strive to accentuate certain components of a scene they are photographing. Essentially, they set the camera on a tripod and then open and close the shutter many times. Each time the shutter opens, they use a strobe, also known as a flash, to shoot light at a particular part of the scene, such as a tree. The extra light concentrated on the tree makes it stand out from the background when the photo is processed.

Painting with light can be used to make a photo appear as though it includes the image of a ghost. Psychologist Katherine Ramsland learned the technique while taking a class on crime scene photography—which is typically performed in low-light situations. To paint with light, she explains that instead of using a bright strobe, she used a flashlight with a much dimmer beam. By sweeping the flashlight across the scene as she photographed, Ramsland was able to create eerie streaks of light on the final image. She says, "I've seen a lot of ghost photos, and it was clear to me just from my initial results that someone who knows this technique would have no trouble recreating photos to pass as ghost photos. Learning about it gave me yet another tool for investigating fraud, which is all too rampant in the [ghost]-hunting community."

Katherine Ramsland, "How to Fake a Ghost Photo," *Shadow Boxing* (blog), *Psychology Today,* October 11, 2013. www.psychologytoday.com.

Ghost Research Society reports that a different photographer caught the same image. This time the camera was a Polaroid SX-70, another inexpensive camera with little capability for trick photography or darkroom shenanigans.

Another photograph that has prompted debate over its authenticity was taken in 1924 onboard an oil tanker, the SS *Watertown*. During the voyage two seamen, Michael Meehan and

James Courtney, died in an accident when they inhaled gas fumes. According to custom, their bodies were buried at sea. The next day apparitions of the two dead sailors' faces are said to have appeared onboard. For several days the crew was haunted by the faces of Meehan and Courtney. Finally, a crew member photographed the apparitions.

Certainly, there would have been plenty of opportunity to manipulate the image, but in this case the photographer immediately handed the camera to the captain, who locked it up until the ship reached its home port of New Orleans, Louisiana. The captain gave the camera to his company, which shipped it to New York City where the film was removed and processed by a professional photographer who was not told it contained an image of ghosts. "The film was developed and printed by a commercial photographer, and there were the heads of Courtney and Meehan, exactly as they had been seen on board ship,"[61] says Kaczmarek.

Still, in the case of the SS *Watertown* ghosts, there was cause for skepticism. After the ship docked in New Orleans, the entire crew was replaced. After the *Watertown* set sail with new crew members, nobody aboard ship reported seeing the ghosts of Meehan and Courtney. Moreover, Cities Service Company, the oil company that owned the *Watertown*, sought publicity for the apparent paranormal incident—even publishing the photo of the two ghosts in its own company magazine. The company's desire to spread the news of the crew's alleged encounter with spirits led skeptics to wonder whether the whole incident was a publicity stunt.

Plea of Insanity

Skeptics have long harbored doubts about another paranormal incident that captured widespread attention when the haunting of a family living in suburban Amityville, New York, was chronicled in a 1977 best-selling book, *The Amityville Horror: A True Story*. In 1979 the book was adapted into a widely popular movie that earned $86 million at the box office. Several sequels as well as a 2005 remake of the original film have been produced, making the incident in Amityville a well-known chapter in American pop culture.

The story begins in 1974 when six members of the family living in the Amityville home were murdered by the oldest son, Ronald DeFeo Jr. DeFeo claimed he had been driven to commit the murders by a paranormal entity. At trial DeFeo's attorney, William Weber, argued that his client was not guilty by reason of insanity. The jurors were not convinced that DeFeo suffered from a mental illness that drove him to commit the murders. They found him guilty and sentenced him to life in prison.

A year after the murders George and Kathy Lutz bought the DeFeo home and moved in with their three children. Soon it became clear to the Lutzes as well as their visitors that a mysterious entity inhabited the home. A priest, identified in the book as Father Mancuso, was the first to become aware of the entity when he arrived at the house a few days after the Lutzes moved in to offer a blessing for the family in their new home. *Amityville Horror* author

A scene from the 2005 remake of the 1979 film The Amityville Horror *is pictured. Although the book that inspired the movies was supposedly based on a true story, the tale of ghostly events in a New England home was later revealed by its perpetrators to have been a hoax.*

The Truth About Amityville

Decades after the poltergeist haunting at the Lutz home in Amityville, New York, was exposed as a hoax, one of the Lutz children continues to believe the family was intimidated by a true paranormal entity. Danny Lutz was ten years old when his family was forced to flee the home after nearly a month of terrifying paranormal incidents. Now working as a stonemason in New York City, Lutz recalls being levitated—cast into the air—while also seeing an apparition in his sister's room. Also, he says, the incident portrayed in the book and film in which the house was besieged by swarms of flies actually happened. And he says doors slammed open and shut on their own. "The entire family was standing there, watching that garage door slam up and slam down, and slam up and slam down," he says.

Danny Lutz, his brother Christopher, and his sister Melissa were the children of Kathy Lutz and stepchildren of her husband, George Lutz. The couple divorced in the 1980s. Kathy died in 2004; George died in 2006.

Danny blames the haunting on his stepfather, who dabbled in the occult and possibly lured the poltergeist to the home. According to Danny, the bookshelves of the family's home were lined with George's collection of books on Satan and magic. Moreover, he claims, his stepfather held the power of telekinesis—the ability to move objects with one's mind. "I just wanted somebody to believe me," Lutz says. "It has been in my dreams my whole life."

Quoted in Tom Leonard, "The Amityville Horror: The Boy Who Lived in the True-Life Haunted House Breaks His 40-Year Silence," *Daily Mail*, March 28, 2013. www.daily mail.co.uk.

Jay Anson describes what happened next: "When he flicked the first holy water and uttered the words that accompany the gesture, Father Mancuso heard a masculine voice say with terrible clarity: *'Get out!'*"[62]

The Amityville Hoax

Over the next several days the Lutzes heard the menacing voice themselves. Soon, even more bizarre events unfolded in the house. Swarms of flies plagued the house even though the family had moved in during December, a time of year when flies are not usually active in New York. Kathy Lutz suffered from vivid nightmares in which she saw DeFeo take the lives of his family members. The family's dog Harry cowered and seemed constantly frightened. Kathy felt the invisible embrace of the entity. Doors slammed, seemingly for no reason. Windows opened and shut on their own. Kathy developed mysterious welts on her chest and was even levitated—thrust into the air by an unseen force. Other members of the family were also levitated. Slime oozed from the walls. Finally, after nearly a month, the terrified Lutz family fled the home.

While these events may have made good fodder for a book and movie, in 1979—the year in which the movie was released—Weber disclosed that it was all a hoax. He said the Lutz family could not afford the mortgage payments on the home, and he helped George Lutz concoct the story with the intention of selling it to a publisher and movie producer. According to Weber, the slime the Lutzes claimed had oozed from the walls was actually spaghetti sauce. "We took real-life incidents and transposed them," Weber admitted. "In other words, it was a hoax."[63]

Weber said he went along with the hoax because he hoped a new wave of publicity about the DeFeo murders might help Ronald DeFeo win a new trial. (DeFeo was never retried and as of 2015 remained incarcerated in a New York State prison.)

In 1986 an independent paranormal investigator, Stephen Kaplan, looked into the case and also concluded it was a hoax. He wrote, "After several months of extensive research and interviews with those involved in the Amityville Horror . . . we found no evidence to support the claim of a haunted house. What we did find

> "After several months of extensive research and interviews with those involved in the Amityville Horror . . . we found no evidence to support the claim of a haunted house."[64]
>
> —*Paranormal investigator Stephen Kaplan.*

63

is a couple that had purchased a house that they economically could not afford. It is our professional opinion that the story of its haunting is mostly fiction."[64]

Fight or Flight

Certainly, not all people who believe they have seen ghosts have been fooled into believing in the spirit world by fortune hunters. Many people who claim to have encountered ghosts sincerely believe they have made contact with spirits and can recount in vivid detail what they see and hear. However, skeptics of the paranormal suggest there may be medical or pharmaceutical reasons behind many encounters with the spirit world.

> "You also become hyper-vigilant, so you start noticing footsteps or voices you wouldn't have noticed before, and start assuming this is some sort of weird paranormal activity."[65]
>
> —Psychologist Ronald Wiseman.

One common physical condition that most people experience is the so-called "fight or flight" response. When people find themselves under stress, their brain often gives them two options: Run away, or stay and fight. Regardless of whether the person leaves the scene of his or her stress or stays and fights back, certain physical changes occur in the body. The heart rate may increase. The person may perspire. The pupils in the eyes may open wide. Heavy breathing may occur.

According to Ronald Wiseman, a psychologist at the University of Hertfordshire in Great Britain, these physical changes may affect the person's brain, altering his or her sense of reality. If the person happens to be in a haunted house or any other place where spirits are said to roam, the fight or flight response may cause them to imagine the presence of paranormal entities. He says,

[There is the] notion that people see something out of the corner of their eye, particularly if they're in a "haunted" location. It's the power of suggestion, as well as fear. When we become afraid, blood flows from the fingertips to the major muscles of the body as you get ready to run or fight, and that can make you cold. You also become hyper-vigilant, so you start noticing footsteps or voices you wouldn't have noticed before, and start assuming this is some sort of weird paranormal activity.[65]

Drugs and Ghosts

Most people at some point in their lives can be expected to experience the fight or flight response—although most people do not claim to see ghosts as they deal with stressful situations. However, another reason offered as an explanation for why some people believe they have seen ghosts is a medical condition known as hallucinations.

A hallucination is a false perception of reality. Hallucinations can be caused by drug use or mental disorders. Drugs that may cause hallucinations include both legal and illegal substances. The illegal drug LSD, which gained wide popularity during the 1960s, is well known to cause its users to hallucinate—often for many hours at a time. Film star Peter Fonda experimented with LSD in the 1960s, and during one experience while on the drug he believed he had entered the spirit world, telling friends, "I know what it's like to be dead."[66]

Even some drugs that are prescribed by physicians and therefore obtained legally in pharmacies are known to cause hallucinations. In 2010 the US Substance Abuse and Mental Health Services Administration reported that nearly twenty thousand people taking prescription pills to treat their chronic insomnia visited hospital emergency rooms. Among the symptoms reported by the patients were confusion, paranoia, and hallucinations.

Spirits and Schizophrenia

Hallucinations may also be caused by mental disorders. The most common mental disorder that prompts patients to hallucinate is schizophrenia—a severe mental illness that causes people to act in irrational ways. Schizophrenics may hear voices, appear to be frightened by the most common activities of life, and suspect

Although scientists offer explanations for ghost sightings ranging from the mental disorder schizophrenia to hallucinations, people who believe they have encountered a malevolent spirit can be terrified by the experience.

others are conspiring against them. And they hallucinate. Said the late Cornell University astronomer Carl Sagan, a long-time critic of pseudoscience, "We know that hallucinations arise from sensory deprivation, drugs, illness and high fever, a lack of . . . sleep, changes in brain chemistry and so on."[67]

But Grant Wilson says he investigated one case in which a fourteen-year-old girl named Allie, who had been diagnosed with schizophrenia, believed she had been seeing and hearing ghosts. Wilson and James Hawes spent time with Allie, recording equipment in hand. Suddenly Allie began recounting details of incidents in local history—incidents of which she had no prior knowledge. Wilson and Hawes recorded her ramblings, then consulted local historians who confirmed the stories Allie had told. "In our view, this was enough evidence to support the contention that she wasn't schizophrenic," insists Wilson. "She was just becoming sensitive to the paranormal."[68]

Grief Hallucinations

Schizophrenia is a serious mental disorder that can last a lifetime and can usually be controlled only with drugs. Most drugs prescribed to treat schizophrenia increase the flow of dopamine—the chemical in the brain that enhances feelings of pleasure. Therefore, doctors believe, when people feel good about themselves they will not hallucinate—and will not see entities from the spirit world.

But schizophrenia is not the only disease that prompts people to hallucinate. Indeed, some people with less serious mental disorders have reported seeing ghosts. Psychologists point out that shortly after the death of a loved one, a person can be overcome with grief and become very vulnerable to "grief hallucinations." Says Vaughan Bell, a professor of psychiatry at the University of Antioquia in Colombia,

> The dead stay with us, that much is clear. They remain in our hearts and minds, of course, but for many people they also linger in our senses—as sights, sounds, smells, touches or presences. Grief hallucinations are a normal reaction to bereavement but are rarely discussed, because people fear they might be considered insane or mentally destabilized by their loss. As a society we tend to associate hallucinations with things like drugs and mental illness, but we now know that hallucinations are common in sober healthy people and that they are more likely during times of stress.[69]

Bell cites one study by the University of Göteborg in Sweden in which 80 percent of elderly people reported contact with the ghosts of their spouses within a month after the deaths of their husbands or wives. These are individuals who spent many decades living with their spouses, and therefore their grief was understandably deep. But others grieve as well. According to Bell, one woman who lost her daughter to a heroin overdose regularly saw the apparition of her daughter and heard her say "Mamma, Mamma!" and "It's so cold." Says Bell, "Thankfully, these distressing experiences tend to be rare, and most people who experience hallucinations during bereavement find them comforting, as if they were re-connecting with something of the positive from the person's life."[70]

Sleep Paralysis

Another ailment that leads to hallucinations is sleep paralysis—a very common yet unexplainable condition that affects as many as 40 percent of people at some point in their lives. A victim of sleep paralysis will wake up and find he or she is unable to move. The patient is temporarily paralyzed. It can be a frightening experience. Moreover, a symptom of sleep paralysis can be hallucinations. Salma, a twenty-year-old student at The American University in Cairo, Egypt, told physicians that she awoke one morning, found herself paralyzed, and suddenly saw the image of an intruder in her bedroom—a fanged and bloody creature. "[It was] something out of a horror movie,"[71] she said.

Baland Jalal, a neuroscientist at the University of California at San Diego, suggests hallucinations caused by sleep paralysis may be a result of a person experiencing a heavily confused period at the moment he or she wakes up. Perhaps, he suggests, a nightmare involving a ghost startles the person out of his or her sleep. He says, "If you have fear, the activation in fear centers in the brain might mean more likelihood of fully awaking during sleep paralysis, and experiencing the whole thing."[72]

Many People Still Believe

Scientists argue that there are many reasons people may believe they see ghosts. They may suffer from mental disorders or see spirits while under the influence of drugs. Or they may be duped into believing in the paranormal by the perpetrators of hoaxes. Still, as the public opinion polls reflect, perhaps tens of millions of people believe in the existence of the spirit world. Clearly, Houdini was unable to convince a lot people that communication with ghosts is not possible. In the decades since the magician's death, many skeptics and scientists have tried to cast doubt on the existence of the spirit world—evidently with little success.

Source Notes

Introduction: Ghost Hunting: Science or Pseudoscience?

1. Harry Houdini, *A Magician Among the Spirits*. New York: Harper & Brothers, 1924, p. xii.

2. Quoted in Houdini, *A Magician Among the Spirits*, p. 184.

3. Jason Hawes and Grant Wilson, *Ghost Files: The Collected Cases from Ghost Hunting and Seeking Spirits*. New York: Simon & Schuster, 2011, p. 18.

4. Jonathan C. Smith, *Pseudoscience and Extraordinary Claims of the Paranormal: A Critical Thinker's Toolkit*. Malden, MA: Wiley, 2010, eBook.

Chapter One: What Are Ghosts?

5. James Van Praagh, *Ghosts Among Us: Uncovering the Truth About the Other Side*. New York: HarperOne, 2008, p. 37.

6. Leo Ruickbie, *The Supernatural: Ghosts, Vampires, and the Paranormal*. London: Running, 2012, p. 8.

7. Quoted in David J. Seibold and Charles J. Adams III, *Cape May Ghost Stories*. Reading, PA: Exeter House, 2003, p. 23.

8. Quoted in Seibold and Adams III, *Cape May Ghost Stories*, p. 24.

9. Quoted in Seibold and Adams III, *Cape May Ghost Stories*, p. 25.

10. Gordon Rutter, *Ghosts Caught on Film 3*. Cincinnati, OH: David & Charles, 2011, p. 16.

11. Susanna O'Neill, *Folklore of Lincolnshire*. Gloucestershire, UK: History Press, 2012, eBook.

12. Quoted in Roots Web, "Todd County Kentucky Pioneers, Andersons, and Watsons: 'Lady in Gray' Martha Watson Porter Still Roaming at Riverwood," May 25, 2005. http://wc .rootsweb.ancestry.com.

13. Nancy Reagan, *My Turn: The Memoirs of Nancy Reagan*. New York: Random House, 1989, p. 85.

14. Reagan, *My Turn: The Memoirs of Nancy Reagan*, p. 85.

15. Dave Juliano, "Why Do Some Spirits Stay Earthbound?," Shadowlands: Ghosts and Hauntings, June 6, 2013. http://the shadowlands.net.

16. Quoted in Joseph Bond, "Vengeful Ghost Returns to Pluck Out Dolls' Eyes," *Weekly World News*, May 5, 1981, p. 20.

17. Quoted in Bond, "Vengeful Ghost Returns to Pluck Out Dolls' Eyes," p. 20.

18. Brian Righi, *Ghosts, Apparitions and Poltergeists*. Woodbury, MN: Llewellyn, 2008, p. 121.

19. Quoted in Alasdair Wickham, *The Dead Roam the Earth: True Stories of the Paranormal from Around the World*. New York: Penguin, 2012, p. 116.

20. Wickham, *The Dead Roam the Earth*, p. 116.

21. Wickham, *The Dead Roam the Earth*, p. 116.

22. Terence Hines, *Pseudoscience and the Paranormal*. Amherst, NY: Prometheus, 2003, p. 93.

Chapter Two: Why Do People Believe in Ghosts?

23. Ruickbie, *The Supernatural*, p. xv.

24. Karen Armstrong, *A Short History of Myth*. Toronto: Knopf Canada, 2006, p. 2.

25. Homer, *The Iliad, Book 23*, Poetry in Translation, 2009. www .poetryintranslation.com.

26. Lacy Collison-Morley, *Greek and Roman Ghost Stories*. London: Blackwell, 1912. www.gutenberg.org.

27. Quoted in J.H. Chajes, *Between Worlds: Dybbuks, Exorcists and Early Modern Judaism*. Philadelphia: University of Pennsylvania Press, 2003, p. 12.

28. 1 Samuel 28:15, King James Bible Online. www.kingjames bibleonline.org.

29. Matthew 14:26, King James Bible Online. www.kingjames bibleonline.org.

30. Quoted in Thomas L. McDonald, "Ghosts in the Bible: The New Testament," September 17, 2014. www.patheos.com.

31. Quoted in Andrew Joynes, *Medieval Ghost Stories: An Anthology of Miracles, Marvels and Prodigies*. Rochester, NY: Boydell & Brewer, 2006, p. 10.

32. William Shakespeare, *Macbeth*, Act 3, Scene 4, Shakespeare Online, 2014. www.shakespeare-online.com.

33. Howard Waters, "Ghosts, Witches, and Shakespeare," Utah Shakespeare Festival, 2013. http://bard.org.

34. Stuart Vyse, *Believing in Magic: The Psychology of Superstition*. New York: Oxford University Press, 2014, p. 18.

35. Quoted in Tiffanie Wen, "Why Do People Believe in Ghosts?," *Atlantic*, September 5, 2014. www.theatlantic.com.

36. Quoted in David Robson, "Psychology: The Truth About the Paranormal," BBC, October 31, 2014. www.bbc.com.

37. Benjamin Radford, "Are Ghosts Real? Science Says No-o-o-o," *LiveScience*, October 21, 2014. www.livescience.com.

38. Quoted in Matthew C. Ramsey, Steven J. Venette, and Nicole Rabalais, "The Perceived Paranormal and Source Credibility: The Effects of Narrative Suggestions on Paranormal Belief," *Atlantic Journal of Communication*, April 2011, p. 95.

Chapter Three: Searching for Ghosts

39. Frederic W.H. Myers, *Human Personality and Its Survival of Bodily Death*. New York: Longmans, Green, 1907, p. 1.

40. Myers, *Human Personality and Its Survival of Bodily Death*, p. 329.

41. Hawes and Wilson, *Ghost Files*, p. 387.

42. Hawes and Wilson, *Ghost Files*, p. 387.

43. Hawes and Wilson, *Ghost Files*, p. 388.

44. Benjamin Radford, "The Shady Science of Ghost Hunting," *LiveScience*, October 27, 2006. www.livescience.com.

45. Kenneth W. Harman, *Ghost Under Foot: The Spirit of Mary Bell*. Woodbury, MN: Llewellyn, 2012, p. 35.

46. Quoted in Deborah Buckhalter, "Ghost Hunters Search for Spirits in the Russ House," *Jackson County Floridian*, February 18, 2008.

47. Robert Todd Carroll, "Ectoplasm," *The Skeptic's Dictionary*, 2015. http://skepdic.com.

48. Melissa Martin Ellis, *The Everything Ghost Hunting Book: Tips, Tools, and Techniques for Exploring the Supernatural World*. Avon, MA: Adams Media, 2014, p. 113.

49. Patrick Burke and Jack Roth, *Ghost Soldiers of Gettysburg: Searching for Spirits on America's Most Famous Battlefield*. Woodbury, MN: Llewellyn, 2014, p. 28.

50. Burke and Roth, *Ghost Soldiers of Gettysburg*, p. 29.

51. Ellis, *The Everything Ghost Hunting Book*, p. 111.

52. Quoted in Mary Beth Crane, *Haunted Christmas: Yuletide Ghosts and Other Spooky Holiday Happenings*. Guilford, CT: Morris, 2010, p. 38.

53. Quoted in Crane, *Haunted Christmas*, p. 38.

54. Ryan Dube, "Go Ghost Hunting with Your Internet Browser," makeuseof, January 17, 2009. www.makeuseof.com.

55. Quoted in James Prichard, "Web Cam Seeks Ghosts in Library," Associated Press Online, October 30, 1999.

56. Angels & Ghosts, "Ghost Web Cams," 2015. www.angels-ghosts.com.

Chapter Four: Are There Other Explanations for Ghosts?

57. Radford, "Are Ghosts Real? Science Says No-o-o-o."

58. Hawes and Wilson, *Ghost Files*, p. 311.

59. Robert Todd Carroll, "Psychic photography (spirit photography)," *The Skeptic's Dictionary: A Collection of Strange Beliefs, Amusing Deceptions and Dangerous Delusions*. Hoboken, NJ: Wiley, 2003, p. 312.

60. Dale Kaczmarek, "Object Obstructing the Lens," Ghost Research Society, 1997. www.ghostresearch.org.

61. Dale Kaczmarek, "S.S. *Watertown*," Ghost Research Society, 1997. www.ghostresearch.org.

62. Jay Anson, *The Amityville Horror: A True Story*. New York: Pocket Books, 2005, eBook.

63. Quoted in Franz Lidz, "Long Island Landmark: Scary Since 1974," *New York Times*, March 10, 2013, p. AR13.

64. Quoted in Righi, *Ghosts, Apparitions and Poltergeists*.

65. Quoted in Stephanie Pappas, "What's Really Behind Paranormal Experiences? Hint: It's Not Ghosts," LiveScience, July 5, 2011. www.livescience.com.

66. Quoted in Devin McKinney, *The Man Who Saw a Ghost: The Life and Work of Henry Fonda*. New York: St. Martin's, 2012, p. 263.

67. Carl Sagan, *The Demon-Haunted World: Science as a Candle in the Dark*. London: Headline, 1997, p. 163.

68. Hawes and Wilson, *Ghost Files*, p. 310.

69. Vaughan Bell, "Ghost Stories: Visits from the Deceased," *Scientific American*, December 2, 2008. www.scientificamerican .com.

70. Bell, "Ghost Stories."

71. Quoted in Bahar Gholipour, "Ever Wake Up and Think You See a Ghost? Here's What's Happening," LiveScience, January 14, 2015. www.livescience.com.

72. Quoted in Gholipour, "Ever Wake Up and Think You See a Ghost?"

For Further Research

Books

Paul Adams, *The Little Book of Ghosts*. Gloucestershire, UK: History Press, 2014.

Patrick Burke and Jack Roth, *Ghost Soldiers of Gettysburg: Searching for Spirits on America's Most Famous Battlefield*. Woodbury, MN: Llewellyn, 2014.

Melissa Martin Ellis, *The Everything Ghost Hunting Book: Tips, Tools, and Techniques for Exploring the Supernatural World*. Avon, MA: Adams Media, 2014, p. 123.

James D. Stein, *The Paranormal Equation: A New Scientific Perspective on Remote Viewing, Clairvoyance, and Other Inexplicable Phenomena*. Pompton Plains, NJ: New Page, 2013.

Ed Warren, Lorraine Warren, and Robert David Chase, *Ghost Hunters: True Stories from the World's Most Famous Demonologists*. Los Angeles: Graymalkin Media, 2014.

Websites

The American Experience: Houdini (www.pbs.org/wgbh /amex/houdini). Companion website to the 1999 PBS documentary *Houdini*, visitors to the site can read a biography of the magician and escape artist Harry Houdini and see many images of the theatrical posters featuring Houdini. By following the link to Special Features, students can read about Houdini's campaign to expose the phony medium known as Margery.

Amityville: Horror or Hoax? (www.prairieghosts.com/amity ville.html). The website provides an overview of the haunting of the Lutz family in their Amityville, New York, home and examines whether the poltergeist was real or a hoax. Visitors can find photos of the home, the story of the trial of Ronald DeFeo Jr., and a review of the work of paranormal investigator Stephen Kaplan, who debunked the Lutz family's claims.

Committee for Skeptical Inquiry (www.csicop.org). Publisher of the magazine *Skeptical Inquirer*, the organization monitors claims of paranormal activity and provides logical and scientific explanations for allegedly ghostly phenomena. By following the link to CSI News, visitors can read several articles by CSI members debunking ghost sightings and similar paranormal events.

Ghost Research Society (www.ghostresearch.org). Visitors to the website maintained by this society based in Oak Lawn, Illinois, can read about the organization's paranormal investigations. By following the link to Ghost Photographs, students can see images that purportedly contain ghosts and also images the society believes have been doctored to appear as though they depict apparitions.

Louisiana Spirits Paranormal Investigations (www.laspirits .com). Maintained by the Louisiana-based paranormal investigations group, the website includes the findings of many of the organization's ghost hunts. By following the link for Resources, visitors can find a page devoted to webcams focused on locations that are believed to be haunted, including the Willard Library in Evansville, Indiana.

Internet Sources

Tom Leonard, "The Amityville Horror: The Boy Who Lived in the True-Life Haunted House Breaks His 40-Year Silence," *Daily Mail*, March 28, 2013. www.dailymail.co.uk/news/article-2300807/ The-Amityville-horror-The-boy-lived-true-life-haunted-house-breaks-40-year-silence.html.

Thomas L. McDonald, "Ghosts in the Bible: The New Testament," September 17, 2014. www.patheos.com/blogs/godandthema chine/2014/09/ghosts-in-the-bible-the-new-testament.

Benjamin Radford, "Are Ghosts Real? Science Says No-o-o-o," LiveScience, October 21, 2014. www.livescience.com/26697-are -ghosts-real.html.

Katherine Ramsland, "How to Fake a Ghost Photo," *Shadow Boxing* (blog), *Psychology Today*, October 11, 2013. www.psych ologytoday.com/blog/shadow-boxing/201310/how-fake-ghost -photo.

Tiffanie Wen, "Why Do People Believe in Ghosts?," *Atlantic*, September 5, 2014. www.theatlantic.com/health/archive/2014/09/ why-do-people-believe-in-ghosts/379072.

Index